Time Tested Thinking

Time Tested Thinking

As It Seems to Me

David R. Wilson

Library of Congress Control Number:		2012914691
ISBN:	Hardcover	978-1-4771-5958-3
	Softcover	978-1-4771-5957-6
	Ebook	978-1-4771-5959-0

To order additional copies of this book, contact:
Xlibris Corporation
1-888-795-4274
www.Xlibris.com
Orders@Xlibris.com
117098

CONTENTS

*This book is dedicated to everyday human beings
who want to expand their appreciation
of the God of the universe.*

Preface

January 2003

T HE URGE TO put into writing some of my thoughts on a variety of important subjects first came to me when I was in my thirties. I seriously considered doing so. However, at that time, I concluded I had not lived long enough, nor had I experienced the cut and thrust of life sufficiently to produce anything that might be of value. I concluded that perhaps by the time I was in my seventies, I might be more qualified.

When I reached my seventies, I had a renewed compulsion to put down on paper some opinions and assessments relating to many topics. I wanted to do this primarily for my own benefit, but I also harbor the hope that others may also derive some profit. I wrote a condensed journal of my life so that there might be some setting to provide credibility to what I have to say. It is entitled "My Life—as I Remember It."

At the least, putting my contemplation into a more concrete form will cause me to crystallize reflections accumulated over the years and thus weigh their worth. At best, perhaps others will be solaced, stimulated, or challenged.

It is my intention to try to present my thoughts from the point of view of a common man (which I am), who has been exposed to the general knowledge and experience available to me as a resident of the twentieth-century Western world. It is intended to be a very personal, subjective approach, hence the title *As It Seems to Me.*

Foreword

A S I INDICATED in my previous statement, what follows in this document is a series of views and opinions on various topics. These are written from a personal perspective and represent conclusions I have embraced after a lifetime of observation, experience, and consideration.

They are not written to present irrefutable arguments to convince anyone. They are not written to prove someone else is wrong or to be judgmental in any fashion.

They are written to consolidate my own thinking.

They are written to stimulate the thinking of the reader.

My prayer is that somehow
God will be honored through this project.

David R. Wilson

Chapter 1

"Is God?"

To put it another way, a person might ask, "Is there a Supreme Being?" or "Is there a Mastermind behind all that I see around me?" or "Is Anyone in charge of all this stuff that is transpiring in the world?"

Another question that quickly must follow is, "If there is such a Being, what is my responsibility toward Him?" and we must ask in the same breath, "What is His responsibility toward me?"

People have pondered these topics in every generation. They have arrived at different conclusions. Some have been released into freedom, peace, and contentment in the discoveries they have espoused, while others have been caught in enslavement, fear, and misery; and still, others have settled for mediocrity, ambivalence, and indifference.

I count myself in the first group I mentioned. I have discovered freedom, peace, and contentment. I want to try to share with you how I arrived at this state of being.

From my earliest recollection, I have been exposed to, and enthralled by, the magnitude and the awe-inspiring, powerful sweep of the vibrant creation around me. I had the good fortune to have an early childhood whose environment incorporated an open ocean, quiet bays, and accessible woods. The combination presented a stunning array of many physical forces permeated by an astounding collection of life-forms that could be viewed, handled, and examined at close range.

It was the coast of New Jersey where I spent the formative first twelve years of my life. Because of its geographic location on the edge of the Atlantic, north of the Gulf of Mexico, it yielded a diversity of powerful weather systems. The variety stretched from placid warm sunshine, to black and ugly thunderstorms, to screeching, violent oceanic attacks on coastal homes and beaches.

I learned to soak up the delightful rays of the sun. I marveled at the brilliant kaleidoscope of jagged streaks of lightning, accompanied by the deafening trumpet blasts of thunder. I was in awe as the forceful, vicious Atlantic surf devoured land and structures from man's principal domain.

During my teens, my residence shifted to Toronto, Ontario, Canada. Most of my summers were spent on the Severn River, which is north of Toronto. The climatic conditions were entirely different from the Atlantic coast. I had access to a small boat, which allowed me to fish, to explore the tranquil coves, to laze in the sun by day, and to drift in the dark by night, as chores and parents would permit.

This environment unveiled an entirely different variety of fish and land creatures than those to which I had become accustomed. Not only that, but as I lay in my boat on the calm waters at night, the star-filled heavens spread over my head and captivated me in their unending splendor. Some nights, the sky would be filled with the scintillating incandescence of green, gold, and red brushstrokes, streaking restlessly across the black canvas. It was the hand of the northern lights creating a spectacular silent fireworks display.

In my early twenties, I was in the United States Navy. I was on sea duty for about three years during WWII. In my childhood, I had seen the ferocity of the Atlantic Ocean as the wind and water combined to crash against the coastline with devastating effect. Now I was living on the surface in a small ship. The waves competed in size and strength, as they churned around us on all sides, driven by the force of the unrelenting wind. They strove to batter us into submission.

However, this same ocean could become as placid and harmless as a millpond. The sun could blossom and shed its warmth by day and at night. The majestic heavens displayed the magnificence of the stars, embedded in the velvet of the ebony sky. The entire canopy was reflected in the silky satin of the surface of the sea. Breathtaking!

Later in my life, I moved to Vancouver BC in the western part of Canada. There I encountered an entirely different topography and experienced exposure to the Pacific Ocean. I owned a powerboat and was able to navigate some of the adjacent waters, which revealed new sea creatures of the Pacific, including the exciting wild salmon. In addition to the sea, the magnitude of the mountain ranges enlarged my appreciation of the world around me to yet another dimension.

I mentioned the foregoing memories because they made remarkable impressions at specific stages of my life. They were among many others that I have experienced, which were revealed through natural elements on every side. They are permanently etched in my memory. They serve as "tips of the iceberg," as clues indicating that there is much more to be learned.

I did learn much more through school, reading, and television as the years have passed.

- The multitude of the expressions of life on land and in the water in so many divergent forms, yet strangely connected

- The indescribable beauty presented to the brain through the magic of the human eye

- The geological structure of the planet

- The sheer magnitude of the universe

- The massive power of the elements that can be unleashed above, beneath, and on the surface of the earth

- The laws that make it all hang together

- Finally, the existence of humans who have the capacity to absorb and to appreciate some of the overall concept

The intricacy and interdependence of it all caused me to conclude that there must be Someone who planned it and who maintained it.

This then is what I believe my responsibility, and my response to Him should be:

In the face of the acceptance of the fact of a Supreme Being of such scope, I stand in awe, and I am willing to submit to His authority. I am willing to admit that without Him, I would not exist. I would not have the faculties to see, to smell, to enjoy music, to love, to absorb the beauty of a sunset, to savor the shape and aroma of a flower. I respect, honor, and worship Him as the Creator and the Sustainer of all things that surround me.

What then is His responsibility to me?

Would the One who crafted my mental and spiritual functions and who placed them in a remarkable human form communicate with me? Would such a Being leave me with a longing to know Him without provision to satisfy this hunger?

Have I been created to wander around on the face of the earth only to stare and to be in wonderment of the works that have come from His hand? Have I been equipped to perceive likes, dislikes, love, loneliness, fulfillment, triumph, discouragement, and the mixture of these and other feelings with no reasonable gratification in sight?

He did not leave me in this disheartening void.

Several times in my life, I have been inundated by the closeness of His presence, not audibly or visibly, but a deep communication of the spirit. However, the most concrete means of assimilating His person and presence has been through the book we have come to know as the Bible. I have accepted and believed that this book is God's current primary method of informing humankind of more details about Himself and us and our relationship with Him and His plans. (I hope to write a separate article specifying why I embrace the Bible as the bearer of the truth.)

A lifetime study of the Bible has opened me to

- a great deal about God's character, by observing His dealings with people in varying circumstances of life;
- the root cause of good and evil in the world community;

- the basis of broken relationships between God and mankind, and mankind and mankind;
- the purpose of creation; and

- God's ultimate plan for the resolution of all that has gone wrong.

The story the Bible tells is a simple one when boiled down to its essence:

- It states that God created everything for His own pleasure.

- He made mankind for companionship with Himself and furnished him with the means to reciprocate.

- He loves mankind and gave him the freedom of will to respond to His love or not.

- There is an evil force at large in the universe that is opposed to God.

- Mankind has fallen prey to this evil force. The result of which caused him to disobey God, and as a consequence, communication between God and man has been disrupted.

- Man's acquiescence to this evil force has violated the world around him and has corrupted his relationship with his own kind.

- God has consistently pursued the reparation of this relationship, which would restore His original intention.

- The price of disobedience to God is death. This means separation from God, who is life. Therefore, mankind is under the sentence of death.

- God Himself came into the world in the Person of Jesus Christ. He suffered the penalty of death in order that mankind may have the possibility of being released from the sentence of eternal separation from God.

- The conditions for mankind to realize the benefit of Jesus's death is to individually recognize his own plight and personally accept God's provision.

All of humanity will separate into two groups. The deciding factor will be whether they have exercised their free will to positively respond to God's overtures or whether they have rejected Him. Those who have accepted Him will lavishly enjoy His presence, which is unbounded life. Those who have rejected Him will be detached from Him and suffer the isolation that comes with the absence of life.

The key to a peace-filled life is unswerving faith in God and obedience to Him.

As an individual, I have acknowledged before God that I need the forgiveness of my sins and that this has been accomplished on my behalf by Jesus Christ substituting Himself for me. He has paid the cost of my redemption. Because I have taken this step, it opens up the promises that are available to me that the Bible enunciates. These promises are what allowed me to enjoy freedom, peace, and contentment. I fully realize that others have scrutinized the same natural evidence that I have and have come to different conclusions.

Some have become frightened and cowered by what they have seen, even to the extent of creating idols of rocks and wood, before which they worship instead of acknowledging a living, loving, personal God. They have not gotten to the point where they have discovered and accepted the Bible, let alone expose themselves to the truths of its content. It seems to me that these people have lives of enslavement, fear, and misery. Still others have concluded that all things that can be seen and felt have come into being by accident. They consider the Bible as a bit of a fairy tale. If they read the Bible at all, it is to mock, criticize, and dismiss it. It seems to me this attitude usually produces a life of self-centeredness, self-aggrandizement, and self-promotion, which frequently results in personal pride and the accumulation of materialism. There appears to be little, if any, accountability in their lives. The net consequence often is mediocrity, ambivalence, and indifference. I find this way of life uninviting and unattractive.

In summary, I have determined that God who created me, loves me, and wants to share His life with me. I accept His invitation. This gives me abundant confidence to live this life on earth and to look forward in anticipation to all that eternity offers.

Chapter 2

Is the Bible Reliable?

I T IS VITAL to me to be convinced that the teaching of the Bible is true because I stake my life on it—now and for eternity.

From my earliest days, the Bible has been presented to me as the "Word of God." I was exposed to Bible stories from childhood, the lessons of which became a major influence in the development of my character. I had complete faith in the veracity and import of the scriptures. As the years passed, I became aware that the opinions of some people did not coincide with mine. I realize that it is necessary for me to be sure of my belief because so much depends on it . . . all that I am and all that I have. I need to be absolutely persuaded that the Bible is the bearer of the truth of God.

I have come to understand that some people think that the Bible is a collection of myths, that it has no more current relevance than any assortment of age-old fairy tales. If this were true, then it would be shear folly to place any confidence in it because life and death are the issues.

Some dismiss the Bible as a nonauthoritative combination of writings that has been adopted by religious fanatics. I can understand how a person might arrive at such a conclusion because of the unbalanced emphasis placed by certain groups on some passages of scripture. However, my reading of the entire Bible, many times over in several different English translations, leads me to conclude that this is an erroneous analysis based on isolated random cases, which do not represent the totality of the teaching of the Bible. Because a few people misapply what is taught does not invalidate the authority of the Bible.

Others approach the Bible as an interesting series of writings with poetical and literary merit but having no moral significance. The Bible is replete with poetic songs, from the song of deliverance out of Egypt (Exodus 15) to the exaltation of God (Psalm 104) to the triumphant song of the Lamb (Revelation 15). It is said that nearly one-third of the Hebrew Bible is poetry. Nevertheless, it is not the aesthetic ambiance alone that is important, the essence is the underlying truth that carries the impact. To have the book stand, only as a tome of beautiful imagery, does not help when death knocks at one's door.

Some hate the Bible with bitter venom. Its message seems to touch a chord within their spirits that triggers the need to respond with energized vindictiveness to downgrade it, to discredit it, and to destroy it. History provides events where people have been forced to burn their Bibles in bonfires. At other times, some have been burned at the stake for their acceptance of the directives found in the scripture.

Over the years, academics have gone to great lengths to create doubts in the minds of the general public relating to the historical accuracy of the Bible. As I consider all of these attacks, it causes me to wonder if there is a powerful spiritual enemy coordinating these activities. If it were only an accumulation of pages stuck together, why bother?

Certain people put it on par with diverse religious writings such as the Koran and Buddhist or Taoist scriptures. The inference being that there are many ways to reach or appease the God of the universe. It doesn't matter which one we follow. To me, the message of each of these is so vastly dissimilar that it causes me to question whether the same God could possibly be the author of all of them. Rather, it leaves me with the impression that several human imaginations have produced a variety of schemes to placate a fantasized god. Generally, the arrangement allows them to do the proper good works, which will be acknowledged by their god, who will then bestow his favors on those who please him. Personally, I would not want to have to depend on my own good works to achieve eternal life. I know that I would fall far short.

Just as God communicates with man through natural life and laws that surround him, it seems only common sense to conclude that He would convey more detailed knowledge of Himself through writing to humans, as mankind progressed in reading and printing skills. The Bible claims over and over again that God is speaking through the various writers whose works compose this book.

The following are a number of things that have been brought to my attention over the years, as I have pondered whether the Bible is reliable enough upon which to rest my eternal welfare. When taken in their totality, it has established a positive affirmation in my mind.

1. The Bible has remained the best-selling book year after year for decades. One considers it important when a book has gained the spotlight for a month or two, or perhaps even has stretched it to a year or two. But when one book remains perennially at the top, it causes one to deduce that there is something very special about that book.

2. The sixty-six books of which the Bible is composed have been written by about forty different writers spanning 1500 years. The means by which this must have been accomplished is staggering. Consider the wars, the periods of exile plus natural disasters through which these documents have been accumulated and copied, and whose message has been preserved from generation to generation, finally to be assembled and presented to the world as the collection we now know as the Bible. It seems to me it could only have been achieved by the hidden hand of God.

3. The number of writers is remarkable. They are not selected from qualified religionists only but a whole gambit of occupations. Reflect on the following to name a few:

   Moses was an Egyptian prince.
   David was a shepherd, a musician, a warrior, and a king.
   Ezekiel was a priest of Israel.
   Matthew was a tax collector.
   Peter was a fisherman.
   Paul was a Jewish scholar.

   Each of them indicated that God spoke to them.

4. As one reads the Bible, the continuity of the message is most apparent. From the opening chapters in the book of Genesis to the last chapter of Revelation, "God seeking fellowship with mankind" is obvious and paramount. As the story unfolds, it is equally

observable that mankind by nature is incapable of achieving the standard required to enjoy the presence of God. The Old Testament prophesied the coming of Jesus Christ to make things right between God and human beings.

5. The New Testament is the chronicle of His coming and the outline of the events that fulfilled those prophecies and the history of the immediate results on earth resulting from His advent throughout the entire story. Over the 1500 years of compilation by way of the pens of forty writers, God is offering to humans the opportunity to exercise the faith He has given to them to obey Him and to delight in the communion that He has planned for them from the beginning.

6. The existence of the nation of Israel, for me, is one of the most convincing testimonies to the veracity of the Bible. Here are people who have had no homeland for the past two thousand years or so, and today they are commanding the attention of the world from a tiny strip of land that God promised them through Abraham, their founding father, over three thousand years ago. Over the centuries they have suffered occupation, exile, and have been dispersed to the ends of the earth, but still they have maintained their identity as a people. Persecution in many countries even to the extent of the Holocaust has not been able to obliterate them. It seems to me that God is fulfilling his promise. There are many prophecies, which are yet to be realized, that involve the Jewish people and the land that we call Israel. The scene appears to be being prepared before our eyes.

All of the foregoing evidence is compelling to my intellect, but unless there is a spiritual content to the reading of the Bible on a personal basis, then the whole exercise is pointless. The ultimate test is to approach the teaching of the scripture with the attitude—"God if you are speaking to me through this book, then speak to me with authority and let me know it within the depths of my being." That has been and continues to be the most convincing argument of all for me.

I have found that when I have been persuaded from the Bible along a given line and have obeyed, I have had peace within my spirit that nothing else in life has given me. The periods in my life when I have not obeyed the direction I knew to be right, have been the loneliest and emptiest moments of my career.

I near the end of my days. As in the beginning, I am certain that the Bible is the written word of God. I discard the notions of those who would place the Bible on par with other religious writings, or who would consider it merely as an assortment of myths or classify it solely as great literature or label it purely as a tool for religious fanatics.

> **"The whole Bible was given to us by inspiration from God and is useful to teach us what is true and to make us realize is what is wrong in our lives; it straightens us out and helps us to do what is right. It is God's way of making us well prepared at every point, fully equipped to do good to everyone."** (2 Timothy 3:16-17, the Living Bible)

My unequivocal judgment is that the Bible is the bearer of truth from God to man.

Chapter 3

Life

THE FOUR LETTER word "l-i-f-e" seems to describe the simplest and most primitive concepts that can entertain our minds, that is, until we give it more thought.

Initially, when we think about life, the picture we get is the bubbling activity all around us, the laughter of children at play, puppies frolicking in the grass, the fragrant burst of flowers in the spring. All of which we take for granted most of the time, that is, unless tragedy upsets the rhythm of events close to us.

The death of a family member, the death of a friend, the death of a beloved pet, or some other similar tragic life-ending incident might cause us to ask ourselves, "What is life?" or "What is death?" The definitions of those two words sum up the most far-reaching complex subject that our minds can contemplate.

Because the scope of our capacity is so limited relative to the magnitude of the topic, we are inclined to recoil from attempting to understand as much as we are able. I would like to resist that inclination and put to use the tools of observation, investigation, and common sense that we have been given.

The goal is to throw at least some light on the subject.

There are thousands upon thousands of life-forms on the earth, ranging in size from microbes to whales. Some are visible to the naked eye, and others must be viewed through microscopes. The multitude of varieties is astonishing, and even more astonishing is the fact that each group is equipped to exist in a specific environment. Life on earth might be described as, "that energy within an organism, which facilitates the ability to function in the environment in which it has been placed; in general, this force stimulates growth, reproduction, and interaction."

Let us test that definition of "life" on some of the life-forms that are readily apparent to us.

A tree is a form of life with which we are familiar.

Consider an acorn. When it is placed in the ground and given sufficient water, it produces sprouts, some spread in all directions beneath the surface of the soil. The multiplication of cells above ground emerges into a magnificent oak tree. Under the earth, the cells expand into roots that arrange a circular foundation that provides stability relative to the size of the tree. In the normal course of events, the tree will produce branches and leaves that will become involved with other living things that share the same environment; i.e., birds build their nests in its branches, squirrels eat the nuts it produces, people sit in its shade on a hot day.

As long as a "life force" remains in the tree, it will continue to suck up water and food through its roots, grow branches and leaves, and propagate acorns to reproduce. All of this will keep it interactive and alive in the environment in which it has been placed.

An oak tree's "life" can be ended in many ways, such as old age, disease, a tornado, a woodsman's ax, or if it is removed to another environment (e.g., to a desert or to the bottom of a lake). When something of this nature happens, we say it is "dead." It no longer is equipped to be in vital contact with its surroundings and it ceases to produce acorns, branches, and leaves. Given enough time, its remnants will decay and disappear. The birds, the squirrels, and humans that enjoyed its presence will miss it.

This scenario is true for all vegetation. While it is living, it grows, it reproduces, it interacts within its predetermined environment. When it is dead, all that activity ceases. It is no longer capable of performing within its surroundings.

Fishes are another form of life that we can fairly readily observe. Home fish tanks, large institutional aquariums, underwater observatories, and television programs provide ample opportunity to look at a wide variety of fish life.

There were a couple of periods in my life when I chose to give a significant portion of my attention to tropical fish. I had several aquariums that provided habitation for many different varieties. This presented me the prospect of viewing them in a sample environment at close range.

Some began life as an egg in the water, which had to thatch before taking its place in the tank. Others were born live from the body of the mother and would have to be instant swimmers to survive. Given proper food and oxygenated water, they grew from babies to adults. Each variety came with male and female members. Every type had its own ritual for procreation. They reacted with one another, sometimes with belligerence and sometimes with social graces.

As with trees, fishes are subject to disease, which could end their lives. They become old. They could jump out of the tank onto the floor and would not survive removal from the environment in which they were equipped to live. When something of this nature happens, they ceased to enjoy the company of other water creatures because they have lost the "life force" within them and become "dead."

This scenario is true for all aquatic life. While it is living, it grows, it reproduces, it interacts within its predetermined environment. When it is dead, all that activity ceases. It is no longer capable of performing within its surroundings.

What is true of life in the vegetation and aquatic worlds are also true in the animal world. Consider a dog. It begins life as a puppy, and with adequate feeding and surroundings, it grows to maturity and survives in the environment for which it was intended. Male and female procreate. Dogs interact with each other and with other animals and people with which it shares its habitat. It too is subject to age, disease, catastrophe, and environmental change, which bring to an end the "life force," resulting in the condition we call "death."

This scenario is true of all animal life. While living, it grows, it reproduces, it interacts within its predetermined environment. When it is dead, all that activity ceases. It is no longer capable of performing within its surroundings.

Other forms of life are not so easily observable, such as birds, insects, reptiles, microbes, and virus. Scientists who have the facilities to investigate more closely the lives of these creatures report, as with other forms of life, the scenario remains the same. While it is living, it grows, it reproduces, it interacts within its predetermined environment. When it is dead, all that activity ceases. It is no longer capable of performing within its surroundings.

What about human beings then? People have many of the characteristics that are found in animals.

Indeed, at first glance, their patterns of life seem to be completely parallel. They are born. They grow. They are male and female. They procreate. They interact with other life-forms in the habitat they occupy. They, apparently, are subject to losing their "life force" by age, by disease, by catastrophe, or by change to a hostile environment in which they are not equipped to live. When this happens, they are no longer able to function in society. We say they are "dead."

In the simplest of terms, "death is the absence of life."

The questions are: "Are people really the same as animals?" or "Do people represent a dimension that goes beyond any other form of life on earth?"

The answer to these questions in my mind lie in the two faculties that mankind seems to possess but other forms of life on earth are lacking. They are "imaginative creativity" and the "capacity to worship."

What does "imaginative creativity" mean?

For purposes of our discussion, I take "imagination" to mean a combination of the following:

- to dream while conscious
- to have the ability to think in the abstract
- to invade a mental realm that is beyond the concrete
- to use the brain in contemplative planning
- to engage the mind in things and events that are not as if they were

For purposes of our discussion, I take "creativity" to mean *"converting what one has the capacity to imagine into something that can be perceived by one or more of the five senses possessed by humans, i.e., hearing, smelling, tasting, touching, or seeing."*

Below are some examples of "imaginative creativity":

- Composers can dream or hear a symphony in their mind and convert it to notes on paper that can be read by musicians and be transformed into sound by instruments, which can be heard by an audience.

- A chef can imagine a combination of food and spices and propose a recipe for an exotic meal, which when cooked will produce a tantalizing aroma and a scrumptious taste.

- A travel agent can mentally picture a vacation to far-off places incorporating banquets, concerts, hotels, ships, and airplanes. She could present the package to a client, who then could actualize the sight, sounds, and tastes of the plan.

The list is endless. Engineers, writers, artists, parents, teachers, and countless other categories of humans engage in "imaginative creativity" every day.

Are trees, fish, dogs, or other forms of life able to do this type of thing? I see no evidence of it.

What is "worship"?

For purposes of our discussion, the concept of "worship" goes beyond mere "adulation" that a dog might have for its master or "hero status" that one human may place upon another. It is the use of "creative imagination" that pushes beyond the tangible that is available to human beings through hearing, smelling, tasting, touching, or seeing. It is pressing into the unknown and allowing the mind to be occupied with the thought that there are "life-forms" beyond the proof of the test of our five senses.

It is the acceptance of the idea that the use of our five senses presents incontrovertible evidence that there is a force or forces that create and control what our senses tell us are there. It is not only the acceptance of the idea but the desire and willingness to give expression in what we call "worship" to the "form" that our creative imagination presents to us.

Mankind has pursued various expressions of worship: from the gods of Egypt to the gods of Asia, to the gods of Africa and the Americas. It is a worldwide phenomenon, which has been a characteristic of humans throughout history. Most, if not all of these beliefs, profess that there is life for humans after earthly living finds its end in death.

As far as I am aware, other life-forms on earth show no propensity for this kind of activity.

The combination of "imaginative creativity" and "worship" suggest that humans possess a *spiritual* component that is missing in other earthly creatures. If this were the case, one would expect one's object of worship to interact and respond to the worship extended.

Assuming that the Bible is the word from the Supreme Being who created and sustains all "life force" (see chapter 2), we should assess what it has to say about "life and death."

The Bible states that God in Jesus Christ is "<u>life</u>." The essence of the energy we call "life" flows from the Creator and is bestowed according to His will.

> **"In the beginning was the Word, and the Word was with God, and the Word was God. He was with God in the beginning. Through him all things were made; without him nothing was made that has been made. <u>In him was life, and that life was the light of men</u>."** (John 1:1-4, New International Version)

> **"So, because Jesus was doing these things on the Sabbath, the Jews persecuted him. Jesus said to them, 'My Father is always at his work to this very day, and I, too, am working.' For this reason the Jews tried all the harder to kill him; not only was he breaking the Sabbath, but he was even calling God his own Father, making himself equal with God. Jesus**

gave them this answer: 'I tell you the truth, the Son can do nothing by himself; he can do only what he sees his Father doing, because whatever the Father does the Son also does. For the Father loves the Son and shows him all he does. Yes, to your amazement he will show him even greater things than these. <u>For just as the Father raises the dead and gives them life, even so the Son gives life to whom he is pleased to give it.</u> Moreover, the Father judges no one, but has entrusted all judgment to the Son, that all may honor the Son just as they honor the Father. He who does not honor the Son does not honor the Father, who sent him. <u>'I tell you the truth, whoever hears my word and believes him who sent me has eternal life and will not be condemned; he has crossed over from death to life.</u> I tell you the truth, a time is coming and has now come when the dead will hear the voice of the Son of God and those who hear will live. <u>For as the Father has life in himself, so he has granted the Son to have life in himself.</u> And he has given him authority to judge because he is the Son of Man. 'Do not be amazed at this, for a time is coming when all who are in their graves will hear his voice and come out—those who have done good will rise to live, and those who have done evil will rise to be condemned. By myself I can do nothing; I judge only as I hear, and my judgment is just, for I seek not to please myself but him who sent me."
(John 5:16-30, NIV)

He sustains "all things by His powerful word":

"**The Son is the radiance of God's glory and the exact representation of his being, <u>sustaining all things by his Powerful word.</u> After he had provided purification for sins, he sat down at the right hand of the Majesty in heaven.**"
(Hebrews 1:3, NIV)

The distinction that is made in the creation of the different "life-forms" in the book of Genesis is quite remarkable. God said, "<u>Let</u> the <u>land</u> produce <u>vegetation</u> . . . <u>let</u> the <u>waters</u> team with <u>living creatures</u>, and <u>let</u> the <u>birds</u> fly <u>above the earth</u> . . . <u>let</u> the <u>land</u> produce <u>living creatures</u> . . ." Up to this point in the Bible's description of the acts of creation, it is as if God were instituting an extraordinary but impersonal formula for the continuity of life-forms, equipped to live in vastly different environments from each other. (Genesis 1)

However, when it came to the narration of the creation of humans, it is a more intimate, a more cherished and treasured action. God said, "Let us make man in our image, in our likeness . . ." (Gen. 1:26) God "breathed into his nostrils the breath of life, and man became a living soul." (Gen. 1:30). There is intimacy and tenderness here that is not apparent during the recounting of the previous acts of creation relating to other life-forms on earth.

This seems to imply that God planned a special relationship between Himself and humankind—a relationship that would not be found between God and other life-forms on earth.

What does it mean when the Bible says that humans were made in the "image and likeness" of God? It seems to me that it means people have been given some of the same characteristics of God, which have not been given to other earthly creatures.

God is the Great Creator with infinite unlimited capability and with unrestricted "creative imagination." Therefore, He is able to express Himself in extravagant fashion. For example, He flung out the universe by the word of His power. God has incorporated into the makeup of mankind that same "creative imagination" (as part of His "image and likeness") but restricted it to be used in a finite sphere of activity, still having the freedom of will to exercise it within those preset limits.

What does it mean when the Bible says God "breathed into his nostrils the breath of life, and man became a living soul"? It seems to me that this, the imparting into mankind, is the essence of the *unending entity of God*. We might call it God's spirit providing the plane on which man and God could commune. It is the platform on which "worship" can take place. It is the common meeting place. It is the area to which man can press to worship God by using his "creative imagination." It is the formation of the "spirit" or "soul" of the human being . . . the id, the ego, the self.

Jesus Christ said,

"God is spirit, and his worshipers must worship in spirit and in truth." (John 4:24, NIV)

If we are to worship God, it must be in the realm of the spirit. It must be real and not false.

God is willing to share His unending life with humans based on the giving and receiving of worship.

What do I mean by that statement?

True worship occurs when the "creative imagination" of a person settles on the "form" of the one and only God of the universe. The fruit of that true worship is conformity and obedience to the known will of God.

"Jesus said to him, 'Away from me, Satan! For it is written: <u>Worship the Lord your God, and serve him only.</u>'" (Matthew 4:10, NIV)

A few questions might be asked at this juncture of our deliberation: "How can so many people in the world arrive at such different 'forms' to worship after using their 'creative imagination'? If there is only one true God, how can humans throughout history wind-up worshipping so many false gods? How did we get this way? Are there other forces involved? Are there extra-terrestrial life-forms implicated?"

The Bible advises us there are other spiritual "life-forms." Many accounts in various parts of the Bible tell of the activities of spirit beings called "angels." Some are for good:

"Jacob left Beersheba and set out for Haran. When he reached a certain place, he stopped for the night because the sun had set. Taking one of the stones there, he put it under his head and lay down to sleep. He had a dream in which he saw a stairway resting on the earth, with its top reaching to heaven, <u>and the angels of God were ascending and descending on it</u>. There above it stood the LORD, and he said: 'I am the LORD, the God of your father Abraham and the God of Isaac. I will give you and your descendants

the land on which you are lying. Your descendants will be like the dust of the earth, and you will spread out to the west and to the east, to the north and to the south. All peoples on earth will be blessed through you and your offspring. I am with you and will watch over you wherever you go, and I will bring you back to this land. I will not leave you until I have done what I have promised you.'" (Genesis 28:10-15, NIV)

Some are for evil:

"For if God <u>did not spare angels when they sinned, but sent them to hell</u>, putting them into gloomy dungeons to be held for judgment." (2 Peter 2:4, NIV)

There is a dramatic scene described in Revelation.

"And there was war in heaven. Michael and his angels fought against the dragon, and the dragon and his angels fought back. But he was not strong enough, and they lost their place in heaven. The great dragon was hurled down—that ancient serpent called the devil, or Satan, <u>who leads the whole world astray. He was hurled to the earth, and his angels with him</u>." (12:7-9)

The narration seems to be elaborated upon by the prophet Isaiah when he is speaking to the King of Babylon, but in reality he is speaking to the "force" behind the King:

"How you have fallen from heaven, O morning star, son of the dawn! You have been cast down to the earth, you who once laid low the nations! You said in your heart, 'I will ascend to heaven; I will raise my throne above the stars of God; I will sit enthroned on the mount of assembly, on the utmost heights of the sacred mountain. I will ascend above the tops of the clouds; I will make myself like the Most High.' <u>But you are brought down to the grave, to the depths of the pit. Those who see you stare at you, they ponder your fate: 'Is this the man who shook the earth and made kingdoms tremble</u>,'" (Isaiah 14:12-16, NIV)

Again, we learn more when the prophet Ezekiel apparently speaks not just to the throne of Tyre but to the "power" behind the throne.

> "Son of man, take up a lament concerning the king of Tyre and say to him: 'This is what the Sovereign LORD says: 'You were the model of perfection, full of wisdom and perfect in beauty. <u>You were in Eden, the garden of God</u>; every precious stone adorned you: ruby, topaz and emerald, chrysolite, onyx and jasper, sapphire, turquoise and beryl. Your settings and mountings were made of gold; On the day you were created they were prepared. You were anointed as a guardian cherub, for so I ordained you. You were on the holy mount of God; you walked among the fiery stones. <u>You were blameless in your ways from the day you were created till wickedness was found in you</u>, through your wide spread trade you were filled with violence, and you sinned. <u>So I drove you in disgrace from the mount of God</u>, and I expelled you, O guardian cherub, from among the fiery stones. Your heart became proud on account of your beauty, and you corrupted your wisdom because of your splendor. <u>So I threw you to the earth;</u> I made a spectacle of you before kings. By your many sins and dishonest trade you have desecrated your sanctuaries. So I made a fire come out from you, and it consumed you, and I reduced you to ashes on the ground in the sight of all who were watching. All the nations who knew you are appalled at you; you have come to a horrible end and will be no more.'" (Ezekiel 28:12-19)

Peter told the Christians of his day that the devil was on the move among them to cause them harm.

> "Your enemy the devil prowls around like a roaring lion looking for someone to devour." (1 Peter 5:8)

Satan has many aliases, even to the point of portraying himself as an angel of light.

> "For such men are false apostles, deceitful workmen, masquerading as apostles of Christ. And no wonder, for

Satan himself masquerades as an angel of light. It is not surprising, then, if his servants masquerade as servants of righteousness. Their end will be what their actions deserve."
(2 Corinthians 11:12-15)

The apostle Paul paints a very frightening picture of the opposition the Christian faces as one engages in the acts of daily living:

> **"Finally, my brethren, be strong in the Lord, and in the power of his might. Put on the whole armour of God that ye may be able to stand against the wiles of the devil. For we wrestle not against flesh and blood, but against principalities, against powers, against the rulers of the darkness of this world, against spiritual wickedness in high places. Wherefore take unto you the whole armour of God, which ye may be able to withstand in the evil day, and having done all, to stand."**
> (Ephesians 6:10-13, Authorized Version)

What are we to conclude after reading such passages as these?

Some of the things that I have accepted are as follows:

- God created a superior spirit of magnificent beauty and stupendous power. He endowed this spirit with a personal will for decision making.

- This spirit rebelled against his Creator and convinced many other spirits to follow him.

- God curtailed his access to His presence but allowed him the freedom to roam the universe, including earth. He is free to move about among us to this very day.

- *He is the master of deception.* He perverts the truth. He has an extraordinary ability to masquerade as other created beings, even to the extent of religious characters. He has the capacity to take up residence in other creatures.

- His motive seems to be, to replace himself as the object of allegiance in place of God, in as many of God's creatures as possible or at the least to disrupt the fellowship between God and mankind. The first account of this subterfuge as it relates to earth and to human beings is found in the early chapters of Genesis. It is also directly linked to the subject we are considering, i.e., "life."

> **"Now the serpent was more crafty than any of the wild animals the LORD God had made. He said to the woman, 'Did God really say, You must not eat from any tree in the garden'? The woman said to the serpent, 'We may eat fruit from the trees in the garden, but God did say, You must not eat fruit from the tree that is in the middle of the garden, and you must not touch it, or you will die.'"**

God had created Adam and Eve and placed them in an environment where they would enjoy sharing life with Him to the full. It was an environment where the giving and receiving of worship between them and their Creator would be the norm. It was an environment where communion and fellowship with their Creator would be a natural occurrence. But it was an environment, the continuance depended upon the use of the free will they possessed. Of their own free will, they were required to honor the Creator by being obedient to Him.

The serpent, through the subterfuge of Satan enticed Eve, and through her, Adam, to use their will to set aside the will of God. As a consequence, they lost the life that God had planned for them in the garden of Eden. They were banned from the environment for which they had been created. They were driven from the garden, but still carrying some of the remnants of their previous life, but now placed in an environment that exposed them more openly to the ravages of Satan, the arch enemy of God.

> **"After he drove the man out, he placed on the east side of the Garden of Eden a cherubim and a flaming sword flashing back and forth to guard the way to the tree of life."** (Genesis 3:20-24, NIV)

- They lost the fullness of life they once enjoyed.

- They were placed under the sentence of death, which would be consummated individually eventually, both physically and spiritually.

- Unfortunately that is the condition in which all of their descendants find themselves.

> **"Therefore, just as sin entered the world through one man, and death through sin, and in this way death came to all men, because all sinned—"** (Romans 5:12, NIV)

Perhaps we should pause to review at this point in our reflection of "life" through observation, investigation, and common sense. What have we learned?

Some of the things that stand out to me are as follows:

- There is a mysterious force we call "life" that empowers "entities" to function in specific environments assigned to them.

- Those "entities" have been precisely equipped to live and interact with other "entities" that share the same environment.

- When the "life force" is extinguished, by whatever means, communication ceases with other "entities" present in the same environment. We call this "death." Therefore, "death" may be described as the absence of "life."

- "Creative imagination" and the capacity and inclination to "worship," are uniquely found in mankind and not in other earthly forms of life.

- Using "creative imagination" and the capacity to "worship," humans are able to penetrate beyond the information gleaned from the five senses into the realm of the spiritual.

- Human beings have been given a spirit through which to connect with a vast spiritual domain.

TIME TESTED THINKING

- In that spiritual domain, there are two forces vying for the attention and the allegiance of every person . . . God the Creator and Satan who rebelled against God.

- Mankind was created to be in close, constant fellowship with his Creator.

- Adam, the fountainhead of humanity, was duped by Satan into disobeying God, and as a consequence, the spiritual connection between mankind and God was severed. The capacity to live in the environment with God, who is "life," was forfeited which resulted in spiritual "death." Though still having the means to continue physically, the spiritual potential has been contaminated in the bloodline of humans ever since.

Let us ask again the question "If there is only one true God, how can humans throughout history wind up worshipping so many false gods?"

The answer seems to me to be found in the fact that Satan interferes between the spirit of a human who exercises "creative imagination" and "worship" to contact the God of the universe. Satan provides substitute gods, and mankind is repeatedly short-circuited in his probe to find his way to the Creator. Humans have a will to exercise in making choices and recurrently make wrong choices.

God has constantly been attempting to attract mankind.

> **"For the director of music. A psalm of David. The heavens declare the glory of God; the skies proclaim the work of his hands. Day after day they pour forth speech; night after night they display knowledge. There is no speech or language where their voice is not heard. Their voice goes out into all the earth, their words to the ends of the world. In the heavens he has pitched a tent for the sun."** (Psalm 19:1-4, NIV)

The problem lies in what Humans have chosen to do with the presentation of God's grace and power. Paul gives a chilling and accurate description.

"What may be known about God is plain to them, because God has made it plain to them. <u>For since the creation of the world God's invisible qualities—his eternal power and divine nature—have been clearly seen, being understood from what has been made,</u> so that men are without excuse. <u>For although they knew God, they neither glorified him as God nor gave thanks to him,</u> but their thinking became futile and their foolish hearts were darkened. Although they claimed to be wise, they became fools and exchanged the glory of the immortal God for images made to look like mortal man and birds and animals and reptiles."** (Romans 1:20-23)

Mankind has repeatedly succumbed to Satan's masquerades. Despite this fact, God continues to love humans so much that He persists the pursuit to restore to humans the capacity to fully enjoy living in the same environment with Him . . . even to the extent of sending His Son to wipe out the blight that stood in the way.

"In the past God spoke to our forefathers through the prophets at many times and in various ways, but <u>in these last days he has spoken to us by his Son,</u> whom he appointed heir of all things, and through whom he made the universe. The Son is the radiance of God's glory and the exact representation of his being, sustaining all things by his powerful word. After he had provided purification for sins, he sat down at the right hand of the Majesty in heaven." (Hebrews 1:1-3)

The purpose of Jesus Christ coming to earth is to equip mankind, once again, to live in the environment for which he was created. Jesus Christ said:

"I have come that they may have life, and <u>have it to the full.</u>" (John 10:10)

"I am the resurrection and the life. He who believes in me will live, even though he dies; and <u>whoever lives and believes in me will never die.</u>" (John 11:25-26)

Having contemplated "life" and "death" thus far and having been amazed by the simplicity and at the same time the complexity of what is available to observe, I find it breathtaking and totally incomprehensible to absorb the following concept that the Bible presents to us.

The fellowship, the communion, the interaction, <u>the essence of life, which was shared by the Godhead</u>, was shattered at the moment Jesus Christ cried out while nailed to the cross:

> **"My God, my God, why have you forsaken me?"** (Matthew 27:46)

Even more shocking is the reason for which this fearful event happened. It was to restore the severed relationship between God and mankind.

> **"But we see Jesus, who was made a little lower than the angels, now crowned with glory and honor <u>because he suffered death</u>, so that by the grace of God <u>he might taste death for everyone</u>."** (Hebrews 2:9)

It was not enough that Christ entered into death. Had He remained under the power of the *absence of life* He would not have conquered death. If He were to restore life to the human race, He must be raised out of death. He must reinstate the eternal relationship with the Godhead, and He must resume the relationship with mankind, both of which the "absence of life" had cost Him. Therefore, God raised Him from the dead. He was affirmed at the right hand of the Majesty on high. He was reunited with His followers.

> **"The reason my Father loves me is that I lay down my life—only to take it up again. No one takes it from me, but I lay it down of my own accord. <u>I have authority to lay it down and authority to take it up again.</u> This command I received from my Father."** (John 10:17-18)
> **"For us, to whom <u>God</u> will credit righteousness—for us who believe in him <u>who raised Jesus our Lord from the dead.</u> He was delivered over to death for our sins and was raised to life for our justification."** (Romans 4:24)

Jesus Christ eliminated the contamination that was introduced into humanity by the disobedience of Adam. He, in effect, became a spiritual Adam for humanity.

> **"For since death came through a man, the resurrection of the dead comes also through a man. <u>For as in Adam all die, so in Christ all will be made alive</u>."** (1 Corinthians 15:21-22)

In order for humans to participate in the "fullness of life" that comes through Jesus Christ, each person must be "born" into the family of God, and thereby, be properly equipped to live in the environment that pervades the immediate presence of God. Jesus said:

> **"I tell you the truth, <u>no one can enter the kingdom of God unless he is born of water and the Spirit</u>. <u>Flesh</u> gives birth <u>to flesh</u>, but the <u>Spirit</u> gives birth <u>to spirit</u>. You should not be surprised at my saying, '<u>You must be born again</u>.'"** (John 3:5-7)

As with Adam and Eve, God allows the decision to rest with the personal will of each individual. If one is to enjoy the fullness of life, if one is to participate in the unimpaired fellowship with the God of the Universe, if one is to be born into the family of God, one must acknowledge that God has made it possible through His Son Jesus Christ.

> **"If you confess with your mouth, 'Jesus is Lord,' and <u>believe in your heart that God raised him from the dead</u>, you will be saved. For it is with your heart that you believe and are justified, and it is with your mouth that you confess and are saved. As the Scripture says, 'Anyone who trusts in him will never be put to shame.'"** (Romans 10:9-11)

For those who respond positively and believe completely, new equipment is promised that will enable them to live in the environment for which they were initially intended.

> **"And just as we have borne the likeness of the earthly man, so shall we bear the likeness of the man from heaven."** (1 Corinthians 15:49)

"Who, by the power that enables him to bring everything under his control, will transform our lowly bodies so that they will be like his glorious body." (Philippians 3:21)

Those who believe in Him will inherit all there is to have in all of the universe and anything beyond. *This indeed will be "fullness of life."* If one can delight in this beautiful world despite the present limitations caused by the repercussions of Satanic impediments, consider the boundless pleasure when these encumbrances are all stripped away!

"The Spirit himself testifies with our spirit that we are God's children. Now if we are children, then we are heirs—heirs of God and co-heirs with Christ, if indeed we share in his sufferings in order that we may also share in his glory." (Romans 8:16-17)

As was the case with Adam, the flip side of the coin is spiritual death for those who exercise their will to not believe in Jesus Christ as their entrance to eternal life. They will be separated from God who *is life*. Since the force of "life" is withdrawn, and since the soul, the id, the ego, requires life to communicate with others, all that remains is unending isolated imprisonment with all else shut out. The Bible gives some disquieting descriptions of this condition.

"For God did not send his Son into the world to condemn the world, but to save the world through him. Whoever believes in him is not condemned, but whoever does not believe stands condemned already because he has not believed in the name of God's one and only Son." (John 3:17-18)

"When the Son of Man comes in his glory, and all the angels with him, he will sit on his throne in heavenly glory. All the nations will be gathered before him, and he will separate the people one from another as a shepherd separates the sheep from the goats. He will put the sheep on his right and the goats on his left. Then the King will say to those on his right, 'Come, you who are blessed by my Father; take your inheritance, the kingdom prepared for you since the creation of the world . . .' Then he will say to those on his left, 'Depart from me, you who are cursed, into the eternal fire prepared for the devil and his angels . . .'" (Matthew 25:31-41)

"They are wild waves of the sea, foaming up their shame; wandering stars, for whom blackest darkness has been reserved forever." (Jude 13)

"This is how it will be at the end of the age. The angels will come and separate the wicked from the righteous and throw them into the fiery furnace, where there will be weeping and gnashing of teeth." (Matthew 13:49-50)

"If anyone's name was not found written in the book of life, he was thrown into the lake of fire." (Revelation 20:15)

So then, "life" does have greater implications than the bubbling activity around us on any given day. It is more than children laughing or puppies frolicking or flowers bursting in the spring. Even the little we have been able to consider, leads to the conclusion that there is far more to be understood than what we can understand. However, from what we are able to observe around us, added to the teaching of the Bible, lead me to the acceptance of a range of important determinations:

- Certain creatures are equipped to live in certain environments.

- Each entity is endowed with a force we call "life."

- As long as life is present in a creature, interaction with others in the same environment is possible.

- "Death" is the absence of "life," and when that situation occurs, interaction with all others in the same environment ceases.

- Humans have a spiritual dimension that other creatures on earth do not have.

- There is a spiritual realm inhabited by a myriad of spirit beings.

- God, who is the "essence of life," is the Creator and Sustainer of everything.

- God created humans because He wanted to have a special relationship with them.

- Satan is a powerful spirit who rebelled against God and who, with other spirits that followed him, are determined to upset fellowship between mankind and the Creator.

- Satan succeeded in polluting the spiritual "genes" of mankind by deceiving the first man, Adam, thereby bringing the whole human race under the sentence of death.

- God sent Jesus Christ into the world to heal the rupture between God and mankind.

- Jesus Christ provides restitution for each individual human who trusts Him. Each person who responds positively is equipped to enjoy life to the full in the environment of the direct presence of God.

- People who do not chose abundant life through Christ will not be able to survive in the direct environment of God and will have chosen eternal death and separation from God, who is "life."

The purpose of God will be fulfilled. The last two chapters of the book of Revelation give a glowing account of what it will be like when all that has gone wrong will be righted, when those who have opted to find "fullness of life" through Him, who is life, are gathered together with Him. A brief description is given as follows:

> **"And I heard a loud voice from the throne saying, 'Now the dwelling of God is with men, and he will live with them. <u>They will be his people, and God himself will be with them and be their God.</u> He will wipe every tear from their eyes. There will be no more death or mourning or crying or pain, for the old order of things has passed away.'"** (Revelation 21:3-4)

Chapter 4

Is There Eternal Life outside of Jesus Christ?

THERE ARE LOTS of people who have never heard the name of Jesus. If salvation is available only through the name of Jesus Christ, as Peter and John stated when they appeared before the Jewish Council:

> **"Salvation is found in no one else, for there is no other name under heaven given to men by which we must be saved."** (Acts 4:12, NIV)

It raises the question "How are people who have not heard the name of Christ to obtain eternal life?" There are hundreds of thousands of humans included in this group.

To suggest some categories:

- People who were born, lived, and died *outside* the nation of Israel *before* Christ came to earth

- People who were born, lived, and died *inside* the nation of Israel *before* Christ came to earth

- People who were born *after* Christ came to earth but who lived and died in parts of the earth that did not receive the news of the coming of Christ during their lifetime

- People who were born *after* Christ came to earth and lived within the possibility of hearing Christ but died as infants before they were mentally competent to be accountable

- People who were conceived and who were aborted before taking their place in society at all

When all these are taken into consideration, the numbers are overwhelmingly staggering!

God has made it clear in the Bible that He does not want any human being to be deprived of eternal life. Let us consider a few references:

On one occasion, when Jesus was responding to a question posed by His disciples, he called for a little child to be brought to Him to illustrate some thoughts He wanted to convey. During the course of His answer, He referred to the child several times. At one point, He said:

> **"Your Father in heaven is not willing that any of these little ones should be lost."** (Matthew 18:14, New International Version)

God said through the prophet Ezekiel to Israel some 590 years BC that He had no delight in the death of the wicked. In the midst of a discourse on "I will judge each according to their own action" He said:

> **"'Do I take any pleasure in the death of the wicked?' declares the Sovereign LORD. 'Rather, am I not pleased when they turn from their ways and live?'"** (Ezekiel 18:21-23, NIV)

One night, a religious leader came to Jesus to learn of Him. The conversation that followed entailed a discussion relating to eternal life. Jesus made it clear that God had intended any and all to have eternal life. He said:

> **"For God so loved the world that he gave his one and only Son, that whoever believes in him shall not perish but have eternal life. For God did not send his Son into the world to condemn the world, but to save the world through him."** (John 3:16-17, NIV)

Peter told his readers of the impending cataclysmic, fiery cleansing of the universe. He advised them not to be impatient for this event to happen because God wants to take the time to salvage more of humanity:

> **"Do not forget this one thing, dear friends: With the Lord a day is like a thousand years, and a thousand years are like a day. The Lord is not slow in keeping his promise, as some understand slowness. He is patient with you, <u>not wanting anyone to perish, but everyone to come to repentance</u>."** (2 Peter 3:8-9, NIV)

After reading statements like those above, one must conclude that the God of the universe passionately wants mankind to fellowship with Him in fullness of life forever. However, an impasse appears to be created when one considers the number of humans who have not heard of Jesus Christ and the unequivocal position enunciated by passages of Scripture, such as the following:

In a conversation with one of His disciples on His last night on earth before returning to His Father, He said, "You know where I am going and how to get there." Thomas said, "No we don't." Jesus responded:

> **"<u>I am the way</u> and the truth and the life. <u>No one comes to the Father except through me</u>."** (John 14:6, NIV)

In one of His parables, Jesus conveyed the reality of the safety, security, and salvation of those who follow Him. He presented Himself as the only true shepherd of the souls of mankind:

> **"<u>I am the gate; whoever enters through me will be saved</u>. He will come in and go out, and find pasture."** (John 10:9, NIV)

At first glance, it would appear that there is an irreconcilable difference between God wanting all humans to enjoy His presence but limiting this great privilege only to those who believe in Jesus Christ. Yet there are multitudes of people who have not heard of Him during the period of time they have spent on earth. Therefore, if they have not had the opportunity of accepting Him or rejecting Him, is God being unfair to these multitudes?

The answer to that question comes from the mouth of the Old Testament character Abraham, when he was debating with God. The incident involved a similar subject to that which we are considering here. There were two cities, Sodom and Gomorrah. Because of their wickedness, God was going to destroy them and all the inhabitants within. God shared this information with Abraham. Part of Abraham's family lived in those cities, and he was concerned for their safety. He began a discussion with God, the basis of which was, "Would God destroy the godly in the cities along with the wicked?" Abraham answered his own question with a question:

> **"<u>Will not the Judge of all the earth do right?</u>"** (Gen. 18:25, NIV)

That is the premise that we will take in attempting to find the answer to the question we have raised in this discussion. We would not expect to find the God of the universe, who has expressed such love for His creatures, to do less than the right thing.

What is the answer to this apparent conundrum?

It seems to me that there are four basic elements in play.

1. *Everyone with the ability to perceive the concept of God must have had the opportunity to do so.*

The following passages of the scripture make it clear that all such people have had the opportunity to discern the knowledge of God:

John, who was one of the early followers of Jesus and who wrote the account of Jesus's life that bears his name, stated unmistakable claims in the opening words of his book:

> **"In the beginning was the Word, and the Word was with God, and the Word was God. He was with God in the beginning. Through him all things were made; without him nothing was made that has been made. <u>In him was life, and that life was the light of men.</u> The light shines in the darkness, but the darkness has not understood it. There came a man who was sent from God; his name was John. He came as a witness to testify concerning that light, <u>so that through him all men might believe</u>. He himself was not the light; he came only as**

a witness to the light. The true light <u>that gives light to every man</u> was coming into the world." (John 1:1-9, NIV)

Paul, who was the outstanding expositor of the overall concept of God's great salvation, wrote the following:

> **"Since what may be known about God is plain to them, because <u>God has made it plain to them</u>. <u>For since the creation of the world God's invisible qualities—his eternal power and divine nature—have been clearly seen, being understood from what has been made, so that men are without excuse.</u>"** (Rom. 1:19-20, NIV)

The psalmist scribed these words after considering the majesty of the cosmos:

> **"The heavens declare the glory of God; the skies proclaim the work of his hands. Day after day they pour forth speech; night after night they display knowledge. <u>There is no speech or language where their voice is not heard.</u> Their voice <u>goes out into all the earth,</u> their words to the ends of the world."** (Psalm 19:1-4, King James Version)

These quotes from the Bible make it clear that "the Judge of all the earth" has declared that he has contacted everyone coming into the world.

2. *Everyone with the ability to perceive the concept of God must be willing to acknowledge and honor Him.*

The response that occurs in each person's heart to what God has revealed of Himself is what matters. Some receive and worship Him, some "shrug their shoulders" and discard God's overture, others flatly reject Him, and others replace Him with substitute objects of worship. As the following excerpts from the scriptures indicate

- The eleventh chapter of Hebrews cites a whole list of people who responded positively to God before the nation of Israel was created and prior to the Ten Commandments being formulated. One example is as follows:

> "**By faith Abraham, when called to go to a place he would later receive as his inheritance, obeyed and went,** even though he did not know where he was going. By faith he made his home in the Promised Land like a stranger in a foreign country; he lived in tents, as did Isaac and Jacob, who were heirs with him of the same promise. For **he was looking forward to the city with foundations, whose architect and builder is God.**" (Hebrews 11:8-10, NIV)

- The apostle Paul describes the reaction of those who were outside the nation of Israel who rejected the presentation of the majesty of God:

> "**For although they knew God, they neither glorified him as God nor gave thanks to him,** but their thinking became futile and their foolish hearts were darkened. Although they claimed to be wise, they became fools.**" (Rom. 1:21-22, NIV)

> "**They exchanged the truth of God for a lie, and worshiped and served created things rather than the Creator—who is forever praised. Amen.**" (Romans 1:25, NIV)

3. *Everyone must have faith and be willing to exercise it.* There is no other way to find God other than through the use of faith. This is made plain in the eleventh chapter of Hebrews:

> "**And without faith it is impossible to please God, because anyone who comes to him must believe that he exists and that he rewards those who earnestly seek him.**" (Hebrews 11:6, NIV)

And what is more, the faith that mankind is called upon to use has been given to each human by God. It is not something that we can conjure up ourselves.

> "**For it is by grace you have been saved, through faith—and this not from yourselves, it is the gift of God.**" (Ephesians 2:8, NIV)

4. *There must be sufficient provision for all mankind to be saved.*

The following quotations from the Bible assert that Jesus Christ has amply provided for the salvation of all:

- When Jesus was starting out on His public ministry He went to the river Jordan where John the Baptist was preaching. The following was the statement John made:

  "The next day John saw Jesus coming toward him and said, 'Look, the Lamb of God, <u>who takes away the sin of the world!</u>'" (John 1:29, NIV)

- Again we refer to the apostle Paul when he says that all have sinned and all are justified through Christ:

  "<u>For all have sinned</u> and fall short of the glory of God, <u>and are justified freely by his grace through the redemption that came by Christ Jesus.</u>" (Romans 3:23-24, NIV)

- A remarkably clear statement is made in the letter written to the Jewish Christians emphasizing the fact that the death of Jesus Christ made provision for every person to be free from eternal separation from God:

  "But we see Jesus, who was made a little lower than the angels, now crowned with glory and honor because he suffered death, <u>so that by the grace of God he might taste death for everyone.</u>" (Hebrews 2:9, NIV)

So then, are we given any hint as to the process whereby the Judge of all the earth arrives at His conclusion relating to the giving of the opportunity for humans to enjoy His presence eternally?

Primarily, we need to keep in focus the concept that God is seeking those who *voluntarily* love and honor Him and whose *actions* demonstrate their love and honor to Him. The Lord Jesus made that plain in answering the following question:

"What is the greatest commandment?"

> **"'Love the Lord your God with all your heart and with all your soul and with all your mind.'** This is the first and greatest commandment. And the second is like it: 'Love your neighbor as yourself.' All the Law and the Prophets hang on these two commandments.'"** (Matt. 22:37-40, NIV)

- He is looking for those who respond to Him in faith that is followed by actions that demonstrate the reality of their love for Him. Noah is a prime example:

> **"By faith Noah, when warned about things not yet seen, in holy fear built an ark to save his family. By his faith he condemned the world and became heir of the righteousness that comes by faith."** (Heb. 11:7, NIV)

- Paul, in his great treatise outlining the result of faith, gives us an element of God's approach. He tells us that if the reception of mankind to God's overtures does not end in love toward Him but in sin, it does not matter whether a person is born before the giving of the Ten Commandments or after. Each person will be judged according their response to the situation in which they find themselves.

> **"All who sin apart from the law will also perish apart from the law, and all who sin under the law will be judged by the law."** (Romans 2:12, NIV)

> **"(Indeed, when Gentiles, who do not have the law, do by nature things required by the law, they are a law for themselves, even though they do not have the law, since they show that the requirements of the law are written on their hearts, their consciences also bearing witness, and their thoughts now accusing, now even defending them.) This will take place on the day when God will judge men's secrets through Jesus Christ, as my gospel declares."** (Romans 2:14-16, NIV)

- Paul also reminds us that our behavior in response to God revealing Himself to each individual is the test that determines the validity of one's standing before God. Not to be confused with trying to do good to get the approval of God, but it is the individual expression of the outflow of appreciation of the person of God:

> "God 'will give to each person according to what he has done.' To those who by persistence in doing good seek glory, honor and immortality, he will give eternal life. But for those who are self-seeking and who reject the truth and follow evil, there will be wrath and anger. There will be trouble and distress for every human being who does evil: first for the Jew, then for the Gentile; but glory, honor and peace for everyone who does good: first for the Jew, then for the Gentile. For God does not show favoritism." (Romans 2:6-11, NIV)

The apostle Paul outlined the entire case as he stood among the idols at Athens:

> "Paul then stood up in the meeting of the Areopagus and said: 'Men of Athens! I see that in every way you are very religious. For as I walked around and looked carefully at your objects of worship, I even found an altar with this inscription: TO AN UNKNOWN GOD. Now what you worship as something unknown I am going to proclaim to you. The God who made the world and everything in it is the Lord of heaven and earth and does not live in temples built by hands. And he is not served by human hands, as if he needed anything, because he himself gives all men life and breath and everything else. From one man he made every nation of men, that they should inhabit the whole earth; and he determined the times set for them and the exact places where they should live. God did this so that men would seek him and perhaps reach out for him and find him, though he is not far from each one of us. 'For in him we live and move and have our being.' As some of your own poets have said, 'We are his offspring.' Therefore since we are God's offspring, we should not think that the divine being is like

gold or silver or stone—an image made by man's design and skill. <u>In the past God overlooked such ignorance, but now he commands all people everywhere to repent. For he has set a day when he will judge the world with justice by the man he has appointed. He has given proof of this to all men by raising him from the dead.</u>'" (Acts 17:18-31, NIV)

There is a "Book of Life," which has been in force since before the beginning, to which reference is made several times in the Bible:

In the Revelation given to John, he cites the following:

> **"If anyone's name was not found written <u>in the book of life</u>, he was thrown into the lake of fire."** (Revelation 20:15)

In reference to the New Jerusalem, the City of God:

> **"Nothing impure will ever enter it, nor will anyone who does what is shameful or deceitful, but only those whose names are written in the <u>Lamb's book of life</u>."** (Revelation 21:27, NIV)

In the center of one of the prophecies:

> **"The beast, which you saw, once was, now is not, and will come up out of the Abyss and go to his destruction. The inhabitants of the earth whose names have not been written <u>in the book of life</u> <u>from the creation of the world</u> will be astonished when they see the beast, because he once was, now is not, and yet will come."** (Revelation 17:8, NIV)

It is possible to be blotted out of the Book of Life.

Consider the following:

- The Lord is talking to the church at Sardis and indicates that He will not blot out the names of those who have remained conquerors in the face of adversity. The inference is that others may be blotted out:

"He who overcomes will, like them, be dressed in white. <u>I will never blot out his name from the book of life</u>, but will acknowledge his name before my Father and his angels." (Revelation 3:5, NIV)

- Moses was pleading with God not to wipe out the entire nation because of their sin and rebellion against God. He asked God rather to remove him (Moses) from His book.

  "But now, please forgive their sin—but if not, then <u>blot me out of the book</u> you have written." (Exodus 32:32, NIV)

- A Psalm of David in which he asks that his enemies to be blotted out of the Book of Life:

  "May they be <u>blotted out of the book of life</u> and not be listed with the righteous." (Psalm 69:28, NIV)

- God is all-knowing. There are many passages of scripture that tell us that we are under His close observation. Two samples are as follows:

During the course of Elihu's discourse in which he defended God's actions before Job and his friends, he made the ensuing remark:

  "<u>His (God's) eyes are on the ways of men;</u> he sees their every step." (Job 34:21, NIV)

The word of the Lord that came to Asa after he had relied on the strength of others instead of God. God was watching and withdrew His blessing from him:

  "For <u>the eyes of the LORD range throughout the earth</u> to strengthen those whose hearts are fully committed to him." (2 Chronicles 16:9, NIV)

The psalmist observed:

⁴ **The LORD is in his holy temple; the LORD is on his heavenly throne.**
He observes the sons of men;
His eyes examine them. (Psalm 11:4, NIV)

- A record is kept of each individual's response to God. Every person is judged according to their actions.

  "Then I saw a great white throne and him who was seated on it. Earth and sky fled from his presence, and there was no place for them. And I saw the dead, great and small, standing before the throne, <u>and books were opened</u>. Another book was opened, which is the book of life. <u>The dead were judged according to what they had done as recorded in the books</u>. The sea gave up the dead that were in it, and death and Hades gave up the dead that were in them, and <u>each person was judged according to what he had done</u>." (Revelation 20:11-13, NIV)

- In the eyes of God, the sacrifice of Jesus Christ was accomplished from the foundation of the world and could be applied to any and all who respond to God in faith in any generation.

  "All inhabitants of the earth will worship the beast—all whose names have not been written in the book of life belonging <u>to the Lamb that was slain from the creation of the world</u>." (Revelation 13:8, NIV)

  "God presented him as a sacrifice of atonement, through faith in his blood. He did this to demonstrate his justice, <u>because in his forbearance he had left the sins committed beforehand unpunished</u>—<u>he did it to demonstrate his justice at the present time</u>, so as to be just and the one who justifies those who have faith in Jesus." (Romans 3:25-26, NIV)

To condense and to summarize the thrust of this paper arising from the thoughts we have considered above, reflect on the following conclusions:

- God created each person with the intent that he or she should enjoy His eternal companionship. As a consequence, each individual's name was written in the Book of Life from the foundation of the world.

- He has made Himself known to each person by many diverse means in different generations and locations. These vary from His creation, to His prophets, to the exposure of the knowledge of His Son, Jesus Christ.

- God watches intently the response of each person to His overtures. There is a record kept of each one's reaction and resultant deeds during their lifetime. These records are referred to in establishing whether or not their name remains in the Book of Life.

- Those who do not respond to Him in faith demonstrated by acts of love and worship during the course of their lifetime are blotted out of the Book of Life.

- The sacrifice of Jesus Christ is applied by God to cleanse each individual who responds to Him in faith, thus maintaining the person's name in the Book of Life. This is in force regardless of the geographic location or the generation of the person involved.

Therefore, it is true that there is salvation found in no other name than that of Jesus, as Peter and John said over two thousand years ago. God applies that name, and all for which it stands, to every human that responds to Him in faith, on the basis of what God has shown of Himself to individuals throughout the ages. Anyone who does not voluntarily reply in final affirmation to God's approach, effectively blots herself or himself out of God's Book of Life.

Chapter 5

Why Evangelize?

THE PREVIOUS CHAPTER implies that God specifically makes Himself known to every individual that comes into the world. This occurs no matter where on earth that individual lives or in what age or generation that person may have been born.

God has enrolled every human being in the Book of Life. Whether each person enrolled in the Book of Life remains registered for eternity, depends upon how he or she embraces the overtures presented to them by God. Those who react positively have eternal life. Those who react negatively are blotted out of the Book of Life, having rejected God, and are separated from God, who is life.

God loves each one and has made provision for everyone through the death of Jesus Christ, who was slain in God's eyes from the foundation of the world. God applies the cross of Christ to all that find Him by faith.

Assuming that this premise is true, God already has a plan of redemption for mankind in place, why then would so many people go to the ends of the earth to proclaim the gospel of Jesus Christ? Many of them literally gave up their lives in the process.

The answer to that question is the subject of this chapter.

After WWII, there was a great opportunity to go almost anywhere in the world to preach the gospel because of the liberation of so many countries. Many of the missionaries, who were ousted from the area where they had dwelt prior to the world conflict, were enabled to return. Before their return, however, they challenged the youth who had come home from fighting the war to consider becoming missionaries in far-off places.

I was one of those young men.

In our churches, the missionaries held meetings where they presented many reasons why we should give our lives to carry the name of Jesus as the Savior of the world to distant realms. Among the arguments offered was "unless the people hear the name of Jesus, they would be lost eternally." The implication was that God was limited to using the present generation of Christians to reach the present generation of humankind with the Gospel. It further implied that if we failed to go on a mission, we were somehow responsible for the lives that were lost. I found this concept unacceptable. It seemed inconceivable that the God of the universe would cause the eternal loss of any individual because of my failure to carry the message. It is because of this teaching that I was moved to research what I have written in my thesis, when I graduated from Emmaus Bible School, "The Heathen, What Eternal Hope?" and in chapter 4 of *As It Seems to Me*. It is clear that the intention of Jesus is to involve His followers in spreading the message that He is "the Way, the Truth, and the Life" and that no one comes to the Father except through Him. He emphasized from the outset that this was His plan. He approached Peter and Andrew, who were fishermen, and said:

> **"'Come, follow me,' Jesus said, 'and <u>I will make you fishers of men</u>.'"** (Matthew 4:19, NIV)

After His resurrection and before His ascension into heaven, Jesus gave to His disciples what has become known as "the great commission." This statement leaves no doubt but that His desire is that His followers should be actively engaged in communicating His person and His work throughout the world.

> **"Then Jesus came to them and said, 'All authority in heaven and on earth has been given to me. <u>Therefore go and make disciples of all nations</u>, baptizing them in the name of the Father and of the Son and of the Holy Spirit, and teaching them to obey everything I have commanded you. And surely I am with you always, to the very end of the age.'"** (Matthew 28:18-20, NIV)

Some notable examples of those who took the directive of the Lord Jesus seriously are the apostle Paul, who introduced the message into Asia; David Livingston, who presented the Gospel to Africa; and Hudson Taylor, who preached Christ in China. Along with many other men and women, they sacrificed their lives to carry out this mission. Furthermore, evangelists are specifically mentioned as one of the gifts to the Church to accomplish the will of God on earth.

> **"It was he who gave some to be apostles, some to be prophets, some to be <u>evangelists</u>, and some to be pastors and teachers, to prepare God's people for works of service, so that the body of Christ may be built up until we all reach unity in the faith and in the knowledge of the Son of God and become mature, attaining to the whole measure of the fullness of Christ."**
> (Eph. 4:11-13, NIV)

Why does God choose this manner of action when it seems so costly, while His present witness everywhere happens every hour of every day, anyhow? Why not let the system that has been in force over past generations apply now? It would be far less stressful, and people would still find eternal life.

It seems to me that the answer to that question is found in two factors. (1) God delights to use people to accomplish His purposes on earth; and (2) God wants everyone to know Him intimately, sooner rather than later. *God delights to use people to accomplish His purposes on earth.*

From the time that Adam broke his relationship with God, God has been taking steps to repair the damage. His purpose in creating mankind was to share a relationship with beings that would choose to return the love that He extended to them. For some reason, He chose planet Earth to fulfill His plan.

Many generations after Adam, the human race as a whole, had turned its back on God, to such an extent, that God was willing to wipe out mankind.

He found a man and asked him to participate with Him to carry out His purposes. His name was Noah. God told Noah to build an ark to save himself and his family because He was going to destroy humanity with a flood.

**"God saw how corrupt the earth had become, for all the
people on earth had corrupted their ways. So God said to
Noah, 'I am going to put an end to all people, for the earth
is filled with violence because of them. I am surely going to
destroy both them and the earth. So make yourself an ark of
cypress wood; make rooms in it and coat it with pitch inside
and out.'"** (Genesis 6:12-14, NIV)

God, with His almighty power, could have disintegrated earth and gone to
another planet to start all over again. Or He could have preserved Noah
and his family, with select animals, suspending them in space until he
annihilated all else on earth and then returned them safely to earth again as
Adam's descendants. He had many options that would not have included
the earth or Noah. But He chose to stick with Adam's strain and to give
Noah the opportunity to participate with Him in carrying out His plan.

It was a great privilege and honor for Noah to be included in God's design
for saving the remnant of mankind, but it was not an easy road for Noah to
travel. One can imagine the daily scorn that would have been heaped upon
Noah for believing that there was going to be a great flood that would
exterminate life on earth. Nothing like that had ever happened.

All the other people were enjoying life, and here was Noah, building a huge
ship on dry land. It was not just a few days that this project lasted. It was
about one hundred years. It cost Noah a large chunk of his life to answer
God's call.

Another of the many examples of God using people to fulfill His purposes
on earth was Abraham. God wanted to set up a people for His Name.
His plan was to bless all the nations through the successors of Abraham.
God commissioned Abraham to leave the prosperity and comforts of the
land of his birth and go to a foreign country . . . and that at the age of
seventy-five!

**"The LORD had said to Abram, 'Leave your country, your
people and your father's household and go to the land I will
show you. 'I will make you into a great nation and I will bless
you; I will make your name great, and you will be a blessing.
I will bless those who bless you, and whoever curses you I**

will curse; and <u>all peoples on earth will be blessed through you.</u>' So Abram left, as the LORD had told him; and Lot went with him. Abram was seventy-five years old when he set out from Haran." (Gen. 12:1-4, NIV)

For the next one hundred years, Abraham wandered in a foreign country that God told him would belong to the nation that would be composed of his progeny. He endured many difficult circumstances as he lived in this strange place—all this to fulfill God's commission to him.

The apparent primary accomplishment of his life seemed to be to produce a son, in a land God had set apart. His name was Isaac, whom God was going to use to sire the nation of Israel. From this nation would be born Jesus Christ, the Son of God, through whom all the nations of the earth would be blessed. It cost Abraham most of his life to be used of God in this manner.

Down through the history of the nation of Israel, there would be many that God delighted to use for His purposes at various times, Moses, David, and many prophets to name a few. Each of them served at great personal cost as measured in human terms.

Before leaving this segment of our discourse, we should consider Mary, the mother of Jesus.

Could God have come into the world in some other manner to accomplish His purpose than through a common maiden? He chose to use Mary and presented her with the challenge.

> **"The angel answered, 'The Holy Spirit will come upon you, and the power of the Most High will overshadow you. So the holy one to be born will be called the Son of God.'"** (Luke 1:35, NIV)

> **"'I am the Lord's servant,' Mary answered. 'May it be to me as you have said.' Then the angel left her."** (Luke 1:38, NIV)

One can assume that the society of her day would have regarded her pregnant condition with disapproval. As a young girl, it would have been extremely distressing. And she personally witnessed the crucifixion of Jesus. It must have been excruciating. She stood at the foot of the cross. She saw a body hanging in disgrace and agony, a body that had been formed within her own body. Surely, she would have recalled the words of the angel when she accepted God's purpose for her.

> **"He will be great and will be called the Son of the Most High. The Lord God will give him the throne of his father David, and he will reign over the house of Jacob forever; his kingdom will never end."** (Luke 1:32-33, NIV)

And here He was, languishing at the mercy of cruel men. He spoke to her.

> **"When Jesus saw his mother there, and the disciple whom he loved standing nearby, he said to his mother, "Dear woman, here is your son," and to the disciple, "Here is your mother." From that time on, this disciple took her into his home."** (John 19:26-27, NIV)

How it must have ripped her apart emotionally year after year, as she fulfilled God's commission to her.

God wants everyone to know Him intimately, sooner rather than later:

> **"Then the man and his wife heard the sound of the LORD God as he was walking in the garden in the cool of the day, and they hid from the LORD God among the trees of the garden. But the LORD God called to the man, 'Where are you?'"** (Genesis 3:8-9, NIV)

This is how the Bible describes the relationship between God and Adam and Eve. It seems to infer that God habitually met with them and walked and talked with them in the beauty and peaceful calm of the Garden of Eden. They knew Him, and He was close to them.

Sin entered. This relationship was destroyed. The couple was driven from this warm affinity into the dreadful darkness of separation from God.

At that moment, God began His relentless drive to attract each human being born into the world. Every soul, by using the free will he or she has been given, would have the opportunity to turn to Him and find His loving embrace.

One of my mother's favorite hymns gives some indication of the association God seeks even here on earth. I quote the first verse and chorus:

> I come to the garden alone,
> While the dew is still on the roses,
> And the voice I hear falling on my ear,
> The Son of God discloses.
>
> And He walks with me, and He talks with me,
> And He tells me I am His own;
> And the joy we share as we tarry there,
> None other has ever known.
> (C. Austin Miles)

Walking and talking with God carries with it the implication of intimacy and mutual knowledge. One of the first human beings after Adam and Eve that experienced this was Enoch:

> **"When Enoch had lived 65 years, he became the father of Methuselah. And after he became the father of Methuselah, <u>Enoch walked with God 300 years</u> and had other sons and daughters. Altogether, Enoch lived 365 years. <u>Enoch walked with God; then he was no more, because God took him away</u>."** (Genesis 5:21-24, NIV)

This was in an era when there was no "Ten Commandments," only the created wonders to draw man's attention to God. Enoch must have responded to God through the things he saw and felt around him. God then embraced his companionship, which developed to the point that God took him straight home without Enoch having to experience physical death. Noah was another one of the same era. Somehow, when the rest of the world was ignoring the Creator, Noah responded to the advances of God, and He struck this deep-rooted association with Him.

> **"This is the account of Noah. Noah was a righteous man, blameless among the people of his time, and he walked with God."** (Genesis 6:9, NIV)

As with Enoch and Noah, Abraham lived in the time when God revealed Himself through Creation. Abraham responded, and God gave him an assignment. The New Testament tells us that Abraham became a friend of God:

> **"And the scripture was fulfilled that says, 'Abraham believed God, and it was credited to him as righteousness,' and he was called God's friend."** (James 2:23, NIV)

Moses was selected by God to be the one through whom He would reveal more of Himself by giving the Ten Commandments. This greater disclosure of the character of God was given to the children of Israel. The history of how this nation reacted to the law is recorded in the historic and prophetic books of the Old Testament.

It was true then, as it has been in every generation before and since, that God is the hungry searcher for those who will respond to His unique individual manifestation.

> **"For the eyes of the LORD range throughout the earth to strengthen those whose hearts are fully committed to him."** (2 Chronicles 16:9, NIV)

> **"You will seek me and find me when you seek me with all your heart."** (Jeremiah 29:13, NIV)

> **"From his dwelling place he watches all who live on earth—he who forms the hearts of all, who considers everything they do."** (Psalm 33:14, NIV)

The ultimate goal God has for those who embrace His overtures is spelled out for us in the final chapters of the book of Revelation:

> **"And I heard a loud voice from the throne saying, "Now the <u>dwelling of God is with men</u>, and <u>he will live with them</u>. They will be his people, and <u>God himself will be with them</u> and be their God."** (Revelation 21:3, NIV)

God has created all things for His glory. The sooner all of humanity, to whom He is giving the opportunity to have boundless life with Him, have crossed the threshold of life on earth, the sooner His objective will be reach.

He has revealed Himself to mankind in three stages: through nature, the Law (the Ten Commandments), and finally through coming to earth in the person of Jesus Christ.

> **"In the <u>past God spoke to our forefathers through the prophets at many times and in various ways</u>, but <u>in these last days he has spoken to us by his Son,</u> whom he appointed heir of all things, and through whom he made the universe. The Son is the radiance of God's glory and the exact representation of his being, sustaining all things by his powerful word. After he had provided purification for sins, he sat down at the right hand of the Majesty in heaven."** (Hebrews 1:1-3, NIV)

> **"For God, who said, "Let light shine out of darkness," made his light shine in our hearts to <u>give us the light of the knowledge of the glory of God in the face of Christ</u>."** (2 Corinthians 4:6, NIV)

We live in a part of the earth and in a point of history when we are recipients of all three of the ways that God has unveiled Himself, through Creation, the Law, the person of Jesus Christ. We are created to glorify God. How are we to determine the action we should take to make this happen?

The apostle Paul addressed this subject in Romans 12:

> **"Therefore, I urge you, brothers, in view of God's mercy, <u>to offer your bodies as living sacrifices, holy and pleasing to God</u>—this is your spiritual act of worship. Do not conform any longer to the pattern of this world, but be transformed by the renewing of your mind. Then you will be able to test and approve what God's will is—his good, pleasing and perfect will. For by the grace given me I say to every one of you: Do not think of yourself more highly than you ought, but rather <u>think of yourself with sober judgment, in accordance with the measure of faith God has given you</u>."** (Romans 12:1-3, NIV)

First of all, we are to offer our bodies to God to be used for His glory. Then we are to soberly assess the abilities He has given us. Then we are to use those talents to the limit of our faith even though it costs us our lives in one form or to one extent or another.

God wants all humanity to know Him and have that knowledge increased constantly as was indicated to the Christians at Colossae.

> **"And we pray this in order that you may live a life worthy of the Lord and may please him in every way: bearing fruit in every good work, <u>growing in the knowledge of God</u>,"** (Colossians 1:10, NIV)

God is at work in all parts of the world at all times.

He wants to have as close a relationship with as many individuals as possible, as soon as possible. That relationship is not achieved through Creation or the Law but through the knowledge of Christ. He wants to have His name spread abroad in the world. Since Jesus is the Light of the World, God wants that message carried throughout the earth. Not that there is no possibility of those in darkness having eternal life through existing means, but that they and He can enjoy expansive fellowship, here and now in this life as well as eternity.

There may be other means that God could use to have this happen, such as to blaze the message across the sky, day and night, throughout the planet, but He delights to use people to achieve His work. That is where the gift of evangelism and the activities of missionaries come in.

> **"For God, who said, 'Let light shine out of darkness,' made his light shine in our hearts to <u>give us the light of the knowledge of the glory of God in the face of Christ</u>."** (2 Corinthians 4:6, NIV)

As we have contemplated in the examples of Noah, Abraham, and Mary, He appears to be pleased to use humans to accomplish His redemptive work on this earth but not to be limited to them. He has equipped different people with different gifts and uses them to His glory, as they are willing to be employed by Him.

So it is with missionaries. It is their great privilege to announce the Good News to those who have not heard or have not yet accepted the fact of the entrance of Christ into the world—even if it costs them their lives to do so.

Just as with Noah, Abraham, and Mary, it can be a very expense affair, in human terms, to be an instrument of God. However, it is meaningful and priceless in temporal and eternal terms for the recipients and for the glory of God.

To be used for God's glory and to further the relationship between God and one or more of His creatures is an entirely different motivation. "The heathen will perish if they do not hear the name of Jesus Christ."

It is carrying forward the work of God in this day and age, on this planet, for His glory.

> **"But we have this treasure in jars of clay to show that <u>this all-surpassing power is from God and not from us</u>."** (2 Corinthians 4:7, NIV)

Extracts from the following words from Jesus sum up the topic for me:

"Let your lights shine before men, <u>that they may see your good deeds and praise your Father in heaven</u>." (Matthew 5:13-16, NIV)

"For whoever wants to save his life will lose it, but <u>whoever loses his life for me and for the gospel will save it</u>." (Mark 8:35, NIV)

Chapter 6

Can We Know
What Kind of Person God Is?

THE PURPOSE FOR asking and seeking to answer this question is to better appreciate who and what God is so that our relationship with Him and our desire to "love God with all our heart and mind and soul" may be enhanced.

The task seems daunting at first glance, but if we use some of the means that we normally use in learning more about another human being, it will yield much that will stimulate our grasp of the magnitude of the person who is God.

When we want to get to know more about another individual, we generally use some or all of the following:

- By listening to the experience of others who have had association with the person in question
- By examining anything the person has made or said or written
- By how this person has dealt with others
- By interacting with the person directly

Fortunately, the Bible presents to us the opportunity to read what others have recorded relating to their encounters with God.

We can observe the things around us that He has made.

We can examine what He said or what He has caused to be written.

Importantly, we can examine how He has treated others in a variety of circumstances.

We can have a personal encounter with Him.

Civilizations throughout history have observed things and forces around them and have ascribed "gods" to represent these things or forces. They have created altars or idols to embody these various "gods" as physical objects before which to bow down and worship.

The ancient Greek cultural empire was one of the nations that engaged in this activity. They had "gods" to represent all manner of things, such as the earth, the sky, rivers, beauty, and love. They erected altars in the city of Athens to honor them. Fearful that they may have overlooked an important force or thing in the world surrounding them, they constructed an edifice labeled "*to the unknown God.*"

The apostle Paul, on one of his journeys, came upon the city of Athens in Greece. As reported in Acts chapter 17, it was his habit to talk with anyone who would listen to him about the coming of Jesus into the world, to provide salvation for mankind. This sounded like a strange new religion to the elite philosophers in the town, and they invited him to meet with them at Mars Hill to explain more fully.

Paul noticed that they had built many altars for a multitude of gods, seeking to honor the numerous things and forces everywhere that had a bearing on their lives. He was particularly drawn to the edifice inscribed "*to the unknown God.*" He centered his remarks on that concept. The God they didn't know incorporated everything that they sought to attribute to the myriad of other entities and more.

The climax of his presentation is in the words, "*in Him we live and move and are*" verse 28. In other words, He is everything, everywhere.

The civilization of ancient Egypt also had a multitude of gods, covering every imaginable thing or circumstance. To name a few: several sun gods, sky god, Nile River god, fertility god, and justice god. They had images and stories about each one and followed rituals to appease them.

At a point in time, the Israeli nation was held as slaves in Egypt. Pharaoh, the leader of the Egyptians, made life very difficult for the Israelis, even to the slaying of any male children that were born to them. Miraculously, a daughter of Pharaoh found one of the new born Israeli male babies, floating in the Nile River in a basket. She named him "Moses." She adopted him, and he became a prince in Egypt.

When he became a man, he saw an Egyptian mistreating one of the Hebrews, and he killed him. He thought that this act had been unnoticed, but one of his own people indicated that he had seen him do it. Moses realized that he must leave Egypt right away.

He escaped to a rural area far from Egypt and became a shepherd.

Time passed and the king of Egypt died, but the new ruler continued the cruel treatment to the Hebrews. They pleaded with God to save them from their misery. God heard their cry and decided to proceed with a plan to rescue them, which would begin to fulfill his commitment to Abraham that his offspring would inhabit the Promised Land. Moses was part of God's plan to liberate the Israelites.

God challenged Moses to be the one to give the news to the Israelites and to confront the Egyptian pharaoh to release the Hebrews. Moses was shocked at the thought of the task and began to try to persuade God that he was not the one to lead this venture. Among other things, he inferred that the children of Abraham, Isaac and Jacob, wouldn't know which god among all the gods in Egypt had given him the authority to act in this fashion.

> **"God said, 'Tell them 'I AM' sent you.'"** (Exodus 3:13-14, KJV)

In other words, He was saying that He was the total meaning of what all the gods of Egypt were supposed to represent, plus everything else for which the Egyptians had not accounted (in effect, the "the unknown God"). He was declaring that He was *everything, everywhere*. It seems to me that it is significant that during the commencement of the fulfillment of His covenant, relating to the salvation of the Jews (Egyptian story) and the early stages of His reaching out to the gentiles (Grecian story), He should provide such a strong presentation of His being "*all* in *all*" in the company of so many false gods. His assertion that He is *everything, everywhere* means that He can be found *anywhere*.

The Bible mentions seven absolute, concrete, basic elements that constitute the personality of God. All of these are nouns, not adjectives, describing substantive primary elements. Taken in their totality, it appears to be the sum of all there is. Anything existing seems to fall into one of these categories:

The Way **John 14:6** <u>Definition</u>: (1) A route or road to lead from one place to another; (2) A path in life course or habits of life course

The Truth **John 14:6** <u>Definition</u>: (1) "reality or actual existence"; (2) being in conformity with the facts

The Life **John 14:6** <u>Definition</u>: That quality of plants and animals that distinguishes them from inorganic matter or dead organisms

Light **John 1:5** <u>Definition</u>: (1) A form of energy that provides information to the brain, and hence, knowledge; (2) A form of energy that stimulates and sustains life; (3) also a form of energy which can be converted into any other expressions of energy such as light into electricity and electricity into magnetic force. In modern science, matter and energy are regarded as equivalents, mutually convertible according to Einstein's formula (energy equals mass, multiplied by the square of the velocity of light).

Love **1 John 4:16** <u>Definition</u>: Love is the emotional force that creates and sustains social relationship between living beings.

The Beginning and the End **Rev. 21:6** <u>Definition</u>: Eternity

Consuming Fire **Heb. 13:28-29** <u>Definition</u>: The final Judge

If we are to grasp, even in some small degree, the totality of the person of God, it is necessary to contemplate each of the individual claims that are stated above.

THE WAY

Assuming that Jesus Christ is God, and as God, He claimed to be the *way* in his answer to Thomas in John 14:6. We can legitimately ask what He meant by saying He is *the Way*.

Part of the definition of the word "way" is to "describe the means to get from one place to another." For example, two of the ways we could get from New York city to London is by airplane or by ship. The thrust of Thomas's question was (in John 14), "How do we get from here on earth to the place in the presence of God that Jesus had been unfolding?" The answer Jesus gave was "I am the Way."

Why then was it necessary for Jesus to be the Way?

The answer lies in the first book of the Bible. After Adam and Eve had disobeyed God and ate of the tree of "knowledge of good and evil," they were prohibited from eating the fruit of the tree of life. *The way* was blocked:

> **"And the LORD God said, Behold, the man is become as one of us, to know good and evil: and now, lest he put forth his hand, and take also of the tree of life, and eat, and live forever, Therefore the LORD God sent him forth from the garden of Eden, to till the ground from whence he was taken. So he drove out the man; and he placed at the east of the garden of Eden Cherubims, and <u>a flaming sword which turned every way, to keep the way of the tree of life</u>."** (Genesis 3:22-24, KJV)

God Himself became *the Way*, the means for mankind to get from the place of death and condemnation to the place where he could partake of the tree of life.

> **"For God sent not his Son into the world to condemn the world; but <u>that the world through him might be saved</u>."** (John 3:17, KJV)

Another time, Jesus said:

> "I am the door: by me if any man enter in, he shall be saved, and shall go in and out, and find pasture. The thief cometh not, but for to steal, and to kill, and to destroy: <u>I am come that they might have life</u>, and that they might have it <u>more abundantly</u>." (John 10:9-10, KJV)

So then God *personally* became the saving force that provided the *way* of salvation to rescue mankind from the predicament of his own making.

The early Christians became known as "the people of the Way." Their lives portrayed something very different after they committed themselves to be followers of Jesus Christ. Their manner of living made them stand out among the population. So much so that Saul of Tarsus sought to kill them.

> "And I persecuted <u>this way</u> unto the death, binding and delivering into prisons both men and women." (Acts 22:4, KJV)

And how is it that these people were able to have their lives revamped so dramatically? It was because Jesus Christ was their source, *the* Way. He explained this as He provided some final instructions to His disciples.

> "Abide in me, and I in you. As the branch cannot bear fruit of itself, except it abide in the vine; no more can ye, except ye abide in me.[5] I am the vine, ye are the branches: <u>He that abideth in me, and I in him, the same bringeth forth much fruit: for without me ye can do nothing</u>." (John 15:4-5, KJV)

The Lord served a dire warning about missing *the way*:

> "Enter ye in at the strait gate: for wide is the gate, and <u>broad is the way</u>, that leadeth to destruction, and many there be which go in thereat: Because strait is the gate, and <u>narrow is the way</u>, which <u>leadeth unto life</u>, and few there be that find it." (Matthew 7:13-14, KJV)

The apostle Paul also had some grim things to say regarding those that miss *the way*:

> **"They are all <u>gone out of the way</u>, they are together become unprofitable; there is none that doeth good, no, not one. Their throat is an open sepulchre; with their tongues they have used deceit; the poison of asps is under their lips: Whose mouth is full of cursing and bitterness:** [1] **Their feet are swift to shed blood: Destruction and misery are in their ways: And <u>the way of peace have they not known:</u> There is no fear of God before their eyes."** (Romans 3:12-18, KJV)

The penalty was death for eating of the tree of knowledge of good and evil. It is appropriate to remind ourselves what death is. In the chapter on "What Is Life?" in this series of meditations, the point is made that *death* is the *absence of life*. Since God is *life*, death means to be cut off from companionship, association, and communication with God. This is the plight in which Adam and all mankind, who are his descendants, is found.

What possible remedy can be proposed for such a massive complicated problem as the restoration of total humanity born into generation after generation over thousands of years?

God the Son said, "*I am the Way.*"

> **"But we see Jesus, who was made a little lower than the angels for the suffering of death, crowned with glory and honour; that he by the grace of God <u>should taste death for every man</u>."** (Hebrews 2:9, KJV)

The cost of providing the *way* back to God for mankind, required a rupture in the Godhead. Nothing less would bridge the gap between man and his Creator. The eternal fellowship of God the Father, God the Son, and God the Holy Spirit must be broken and then repaired. Then all mankind could be invited individually to return via this *way*.

Jesus said:

"I am the good shepherd, and know my sheep, and am known of mine. As the Father knoweth me, even so know I the Father: and <u>I lay down my life for the sheep.</u> And other sheep I have, which are not of this fold: them also I must bring, and they shall hear my voice; and there shall be one fold, and one shepherd. Therefore doth my Father love me, because <u>I lay down my life, that I might take it again. No man taketh it from me, but I lay it down of myself. I have power to lay it down, and I have power to take it again.</u> This commandment have I received of my Father. (John 10:14-18, KJV)

This dreadful event took place on the cross:

"And about the ninth hour Jesus cried with a loud voice, saying, Eli, Eli, lama sabachthani? that is to say, My God, my God, <u>why hast thou forsaken me?</u>" (Matthew 27:46, KJV)

Jesus took back His life again:

"Now upon the first day of the week, very early in the morning, they came unto the sepulchre, bringing the spices which they had prepared, and certain others with them. And they found the stone rolled away from the sepulchre. And they entered in, and found not the body of the Lord Jesus. And it came to pass, as they were much perplexed thereabout, behold, two men stood by them in shining garments: And as they were afraid, and bowed down their faces to the earth, they said unto them, <u>Why seek ye the living among the dead? He is not here, but is risen</u>: remember how he spake unto you when he was yet in Galilee." (Luke 24:1-6, KJV)

He specifically appeared to Thomas, who originally asked the question in John 14, "How can we know the way?" Jesus answered, "*I am the Way.*"

"And after eight days again his disciples were within, and Thomas with them: then came Jesus, the doors being shut, and stood in the midst, and said, Peace be unto you. <u>Then saith he to Thomas, Reach hither thy finger, and behold my</u>

hands; and reach hither thy hand, and thrust it into my side: and be not faithless, but believing. And Thomas answered and said unto him, My Lord and my God. Jesus saith unto him, Thomas, because thou hast seen me, thou hast believed: blessed are they that have not seen, and yet have believed."
(John 20:21-29, KJV)

There will no longer be the need for the application of the death penalty:

"But every man in his own order: Christ the first fruits; afterward they that are Christ's at his coming. Then cometh the end, when he shall have delivered up the kingdom to God, even the Father; when he shall have put down all rule and all authority and power. for he must reign, till he hath put all enemies under his feet. The last enemy that shall be destroyed is death. For he hath put all things under his feet. But when he saith all things are put under him, it is manifest that he is excepted, which did put all things under him. And when all things shall be subdued unto him, then shall the Son also himself be subject unto him that put all things under him, that God may be all in all." (1 Corinthians 15:20-28, KJV)

In the fullness of time, there will be no need for the death penalty to be imposed ever again because all beings to whom He has given life and who have entered *the way* will enjoy boundless life. The total fellowship with God, His intent from the beginning, starting with Adam, will have achieved unbroken fellowship between God and mankind.

"And I saw a new heaven and a new earth: for the first heaven and the first earth were passed away; and there was no more sea. ² And I John saw the holy city, new Jerusalem, coming down from God out of heaven, prepared as a bride adorned for her husband. ³ And I heard a great voice out of heaven saying, Behold, the tabernacle of God is with men, and he will dwell with them, and they shall be his people, and God himself shall be with them, and be their God. ⁴ And God shall wipe away all tears from their eyes; and there shall be no more death, neither sorrow, nor crying, neither shall there

be any more pain: for <u>the former things are passed away.</u>"
(Revelation 21:1-4, KJV)

What are some of the characteristics of God we can learn from our meditation of God being the *Way*?

—*God passionately loves mankind* and will go to any length to have a close relationship with any individual that responds positively by faith to His overtures.

> **"But without faith it is impossible to please him: <u>for he that cometh to God must believe that he is, and that he is a rewarder of them that diligently seek him</u>."** (Hebrews 11:6, KJV)

—*God has a plan* and sticks tenaciously to it until it is completed.

> **"And we know that all things work together for good to them that love God, to them <u>who are the called according to his purpose</u>."** (Romans 8:28, KJV)

—*God is gracious and patient* and will not force anyone into the *way*. He has offered His *way* of salvation to every generation of humans from Adam until today and will continue until the end of time.

> **"The Lord is not slack concerning his promise, as some men count slackness; but <u>is longsuffering to us-ward, not willing that any should perish, but that all should come to repentance</u>."** (2 Peter 3:9, KJV)

> **"<u>Forasmuch as ye know that ye were not redeemed with corruptible things, as silver and gold,</u> from your vain conversation received by tradition from your fathers; <u>But with the precious blood of Christ,</u> as of a lamb without blemish and without spot: Who Verily was foreordained before the foundation of the world, but was manifest in these last times for you, Who by him do believe in God, that raised him up from the dead, and gave him glory; that your faith and hope might be in God."** (1 Peter 1:18-21, KJV)

THE TRUTH

Pilate, the Roman governor, posed the question "What is truth?" during his interrogation of Jesus Christ. It is not clear how he meant the question. Was it said flippantly, "What does it matter what the truth is? Who cares?" Or was it a sincere question from one who did not know what the truth was and desired to know?

The query arose out of the interrogation of whether Jesus was a king or not. After Jesus clarified that His kingdom was not of the current political scene, He said that He was here to witness to the truth.

> **"Pilate entered into the judgment hall again, and called Jesus, and said unto him, Art thou the King of the Jews? Jesus answered him, Sayest thou this thing of thyself, or did others tell it thee of me? Pilate answered, Am I a Jew? Thine own nation and the chief priests have delivered thee unto me: what hast thou done? Jesus answered, My kingdom is not of this world: if my kingdom were of this world, then would my servants fight, that I should not be delivered to the Jews: but now is my kingdom not from hence. Pilate therefore said unto him, Art thou a king then? Jesus answered, Thou sayest that I am a king. To this end was I born, and for this cause came I into the world, that I should bear witness unto the truth. Every one that is of the truth heareth my voice."**
> (John 18:32-38, KJV)

Since our meditation is concerned with the claim that a description given for one of the basic elements of what God is like is *truth*, we should clarify what we mean by the word.

The Truth John 14:6 Definition: (1) "reality or actual existence"; (2) "being in conformity with the facts"

The essential meaning of the word is "that which is *real* or *reality*."

In the passage above (John 18), Jesus makes the statement that He has come into the world to *bear witness to the truth*. In other words, He has come to present to the people with whom He spoke *reality*. It was His purpose to differentiate between what is false and what is authentic.

The question whether Jesus was a king or not was the subject under discussion. Jesus did not deny that He was a King, but that He was not a king of the current political world. The fact was and is, He is the King in reality of the entire world and was testifying to that fact.

The time for Him to assume His authority was not when He stood before Pilate but in a day yet to come.

> "**When the Son of man shall come in his glory**, and all the holy angels with him, **then shall he sit upon the throne of his glory:** And **before him shall be gathered all nations:** and he shall separate them one from another, as a shepherd divideth his sheep from the goats: And he shall set the sheep on his right hand, but the goats on the left. **Then shall the King say** unto them on his right hand, Come, ye blessed of my Father, **inherit the kingdom prepared for you from the foundation of the world.**" (Matthew 25:31-34, KJV)

His coming rule was prophesied in the Old Testament:

> "**For unto us a child is born, unto us a son is given: and the government shall be upon his shoulder:** and his name shall be called **Wonderful, Counsellor, The mighty God, The everlasting Father, The Prince of Peace. Of the increase of his government and peace there shall be no end, upon the throne of David, and upon his kingdom,** to order it, and to establish it with judgment and with justice from henceforth even **forever.** The zeal of the LORD of hosts will perform this." (Isaiah 9:6-7, KJV)

The theme is echoed in the New Testament:

> "**That at the name of Jesus every knee should bow, of things in heaven, and things in earth, and things under the earth;** *11* **And that every tongue should confess that Jesus Christ is**

Lord, to the glory of God the Father." (Philippians 2:10-11, KJV)

The finale is described for us in Revelation:

> "**After this I beheld, and, lo, a great multitude, which no man could number, <u>of all nations</u>, and kindreds, and people, and tongues, <u>stood before the throne,</u> and before the Lamb, clothed with white robes, and palms in their hands; ¹⁰ And cried with a loud voice, saying, <u>Salvation to our God which sitteth upon the throne</u>, and unto the Lamb.**" (Revelation 7:9-10, KJV)

The reality or truth regarding the subject of political power is that God will not rule directly over the affairs of men until a future date; nevertheless, even today, as in the past, He maintains an influence on who reigns among mankind as stated repeatedly in the Old Testament. In Jeremiah 27, in the course of chastising Israel, He declares that He is going to place them in the hands of Babylon. He makes this declaration:

> **I have made the earth, the man and the beast that are upon the ground, by my great power and by my outstretched arm, and <u>have given it unto whom it seemed meet unto me</u>.**" (Jeremiah 27:5, KJV)

The *reality* today is made clear by the apostle Paul:

> "**Let every soul be subject unto the higher powers. <u>For there is no power but of God: the powers that be are ordained of God</u>.**" (Romans 13:1, KJV)

The truth is: God controls who gains control of political power throughout the world at all times.

Another concept to which the Lord Jesus attached His witness as being the truth is the reality that He will be the dividing factor among the people of the earth. What one may think of Him, as one passes through this life, will affect that person's standing in eternity. It will be paramount to all other considerations, even that of family ties.

"Fear ye not therefore, ye are of more value than many sparrows. Whosoever therefore shall confess me before men, him will I confess also before my Father which is in heaven. But whosoever shall deny me before men, him will I also before my Father which is in heaven. Think not that I am come to send peace on earth: I came not to send peace, but a sword. For I am come to set a man at variance against his father, and the daughter against her mother, and the daughter in law against her mother in law. And a man's foes shall be they of his own household." (Matthew 10:31-36, KJV)

The deliverance from eternal condemnation hangs on the reception of Jesus Christ by the individual or the rejection of Jesus Christ by the individual:

"That whosoever believeth in him should not perish, but have eternal life. For God so loved the world, that he gave his only begotten Son, that whosoever believeth in him should not perish, but have everlasting life For God sent not his Son into the world to condemn the world; but that the world through him might be saved. He that believeth on him is not condemned: but he that believeth not is condemned already, because he hath not believed in the name of the only begotten Son of God[1]." John 3:15-18 AV

To humanize the reality to which He is attesting, the Lord Jesus tells a story:

"And there was a certain beggar named Lazarus, which was laid at his gate, full of sores, And desiring to be fed with the crumbs which fell from the rich man's table: moreover the dogs came and licked his sores. And it came to pass, that the beggar died, and was carried by the angels into Abraham's bosom: the rich man also died, and was buried; And in hell he lift up his eyes, being in torments, and seeth Abraham afar off, and Lazarus in his bosom. And he cried and said, Father Abraham, have mercy on me, and send Lazarus, that he may dip the tip of his finger in water, and cool my tongue; for I am tormented in this flame. But Abraham said, Son, remember that thou in thy lifetime receivedst thy

good things, and likewise Lazarus evil things: but now he is comforted, and thou art tormented." (Luke 16:20-25, KJV)

The challenge of life for each human being is the same as it was for the religious leaders that Jesus confronted. The major antagonist and bender of the minds of people is Satan in whom there is no truth:

"**But now ye seek to kill me, <u>a man that hath told you the truth,</u> which I have heard of God: this did not Abraham. Ye do the deeds of your father. Then said they to him, we be not born of fornication; we have one Father, even God. Jesus said unto them, If God were your Father, ye would love me: for I proceeded forth and came from God came I of not myself, but he sent me. Why do ye not understand my speech? Even because ye cannot hear my word. Ye are of your father the devil, and the lusts of your father ye will do. He was a murderer from the beginning, and <u>abode not in the truth, because there is no truth in him.</u> But now ye seek to kill me, <u>a man that hath told you the truth,</u> which I have heard of God: this did not Abraham. Ye do the deeds of your father. Then said they to him, We be not born of fornication; we have one Father, even God. Jesus said unto them, If God were your Father, ye would love me: for I proceeded forth and came from God; neither came I of myself, but he sent me. Why do ye not understand my speech? even because ye cannot hear my word. Ye are of your father the devil, and the lusts of your father ye will do. He was a murderer from the beginning, and <u>abode not in the truth, because there is no truth in him</u>. When he speaketh a lie, he speaketh of his own: <u>for he is a liar, and the father of it</u>. And <u>because I tell you the truth, ye believe me not</u>.**" (John 8:40-45, KJV)

The Lord Jesus in clarifying the truth relating to the final destiny of human souls made it clear:

There is heaven; there is a hell
There is life; there is death
A narrow way; a broad way
Salvation; condemnation

"Enter ye in at the strait gate: for wide is the gate, and broad is the way, that leadeth to destruction, and many there be which go in thereat: Because strait is the gate, and narrow is the way, which leadeth unto life, and few there be that find it." (Matthew 7:13-14, KJV)

The Lord Jesus in his discourse with the disciples before He was crucified told them that the Comforter would come, *who is the Spirit of Truth,* and would *lead them into all truth* in His absence. God's witness to the truth in our day and age is the Holy Spirit. It is He to whom we should turn for guidance in understanding the reality of anything with which we are faced. He is present with us at all times.

Jesus indicated in the passage John 15 and 16, some of the things with which the Holy Spirit would be occupied here on earth during Christ's absence:

Convicting the world of sin
Convicting the world of righteousness
Convicting the world of judgment
Testifying of Jesus Christ

"But when the Comforter is come, whom I will send unto you from the Father, even the Spirit of truth, which proceedeth from the Father, he shall testify of me." (John 15:26, KJV)

"Nevertheless I tell you the truth; It is expedient for you that I go away: for if I go not away, the Comforter will not come unto you; but if I depart, I will send him unto you. And when he is come, he will reprove the world of sin, and of righteousness, and of judgment: Of sin, because they believe not on me; Of righteousness, because I go to my Father, and ye see me no more; Of judgment, because the prince of this world is judged. I have yet many things to say unto you, but ye cannot bear them now. Howbeit when he, the Spirit of truth, is come, he will guide you into all truth: for he shall not speak of. himself; but whatsoever he shall hear, that shall he speak: and he will shew you things to come. He shall glorify me: for he shall receive of mine, and shall

shew it unto you. All things that the Father hath are mine: therefore said I, that he shall take of mine, and shall shew it unto you." (John 16:1-16, KJV)

After His resurrection and ascension, the Holy Spirit made His presence known to the followers of Jesus Christ and His work began:

> **"And when the day of Pentecost was fully come, they were all with one accord in one place. And suddenly there came a sound from heaven as of a rushing mighty wind, and it filled all the house where they were sitting. And there appeared unto them cloven tongues like as of fire, and it sat upon each of them. And <u>they were all filled with the Holy Ghost</u>, and began to speak with other tongues, as the Spirit gave them utterance."** (Acts 2:104, KJV)

In the Old Testament, God is repeatedly associated with the *truth* combined with mercy. King David of whom it is said, "He was a man after God's own heart," declared in one of his Psalms:

> **"I will praise thee, O LORD, among the people: and I will sing praises unto thee among the nations. ⁴ For <u>thy mercy is great above the heavens: and thy truth reacheth unto the clouds</u>."** (Psalm 108:3-4 KJV)

Some of the *reality* that we learn regarding what God is like as we consider Him as *truth* are as follows:

- He intends to take direct control over the affairs of the nations of the world at a time in the future, and He has the power to do so.

- He takes personal interest in the current political leadership of the nations of the world and has the power to place whomever He will in positions of authority.

- He will preside over the eternal destiny of each human being, and he has the power to do so.

- He is currently active in the affairs of men through the Holy Spirit, convicting of sin, righteous, and judgment.

- He will guide His children on earth to the truth in any situation.

Jesus Christ said:

> **"And ye shall <u>know the truth</u>, and the <u>truth shall make you free</u>."** (John 8:32, KJV)

> **"If the Son therefore shall make you free, ye shall be free indeed."** (John 8:36, KJV)

When the believer faces up to the *truth*, the *reality* that God is in charge of all things, it brings freedom that nothing else can. To personally know the One who supervises the leaders of all the nations of the world and who at the same time is interested in the eternal welfare of every human being and who lends abundant mercy with the exercise of truth and who stands ready to guide each one into the truth of every situation we face, "we shall be free indeed."

<u>The Life</u>

John 14:6

<u>Definition</u>: That quality of plants and animals that distinguishes them from inorganic matter or dead organisms

One might expect for such a big event as the creation of the universe. God would organize something like a massive bonfire, surrounded by all the spirit beings in existence at the time, and fire off an exotic explosion each occasion a new form of life was created . . . but no. The Bible recorded that He just . . . spoke!

When He brought into existence the myriad types of grasses and grains; when He fashioned the multitude of varieties of fruit trees; when He formed the countless types of evergreens added to the endless diversity of deciduous trees, all having the capacity to reproduce and multiply:

God <u>said</u>, "Let the <u>earth bring forth grass, the herb yielding seed, and the fruit tree yielding fruit</u> after his kind, whose seed is in itself, upon the earth: and it was so. And the earth brought forth grass, and herb yielding seed after his kind, and the tree yielding fruit, whose seed was in itself, after his kind: and God saw that it was good." (Genesis 1:11-12, KJV)

When He brought into existence the myriad types of whales and fish; when He fashioned the multitude of varieties of shellfish shrimp and plankton; when He formed the countless types of fowls, from sparrows to eagles, all having the capacity to reproduce and multiply:

God <u>said</u>, "Let the <u>waters bring forth abundantly the moving creature that hath life, and fowl that may fly above the earth</u> in the open firmament of heaven. And God created great whales, and every living creature that moveth, which brought forth abundantly, after their kind, and every winged fowl after his kind: and God saw that it was good. And God blessed them, saying, Be fruitful, and multiply, and fill the waters in the seas, and let fowl multiply in the earth. And the evening and the morning were the fifth day." (Genesis 1:20-22, KJV)

When He brought into existence the myriad types of cattle, canine, and cats; when He fashioned the multitude of varieties of snakes, lizards, and insects; when He formed the countless types of bacteria, all having the capacity to reproduce and multiply:

God <u>said</u>, "<u>Let the earth bring forth the living creature after his kind, cattle, and creeping thing, and beast of the earth after his kind: and it was so.</u> And God made the beast of the earth after his kind, and cattle after their kind, and everything that creepeth upon the earth after his kind: and God saw that it was good." (Genesis 1:24-25, KJV)

When He brought into existence human beings, with the myriad types of personalities; When He fashioned the multitude of varieties of physical appearances, formed the countless types of individual talents and yet maintained the image of God, all having the capacity to reproduce and multiply:

> **God <u>said</u>, <u>"Let us make man in our image, after our likeness:</u> and let them have dominion over the fish of the sea, and over the fowl of the air, and over the cattle, and over all the earth, and over every creeping thing that creepeth upon the earth."** (Genesis 1:26-27, KJV)

The inspired introduction the apostle John gives, as he presents the Lord Jesus Christ to his readers, continues the image of God as the *Word*. It is through the *Word* that everything that was made was made. He is the source of the *life and the light of men.*

> **"In the beginning was the Word, and the Word was with God, and the Word was God. The same was in the beginning with God. <u>All things were made by him</u>; and without him was not anything made that was made. In <u>him was life; and the life was the light of men</u>."** (John 1:1-3)

The letter to the Hebrew Christians was written at a time when their commitment to Christ was being intensely challenged. The stature and power of God in Christ was being questioned. The confirming facts relating to His mighty supremacy were affirmed in no uncertain fashion.

The inspired declaration is made, "*upholding all things* by the *word* of His power." Not only were all things created by merely *speaking*, but all life, each and every living thing, is *being sustained* moment by moment by the *word* of His power:

> **"God, who at sundry times and in divers manners spake in time past unto the fathers by the prophets, Hath in these last days spoken unto us by his Son, whom he hath appointed heir of all things, <u>by whom also he made the worlds;</u> Who being the brightness of his glory, and the express IMAGE of his person, and <u>upholding all things by the word of his power,</u> when he had by himself purged our sins, sat down on the right hand of the Majesty on high."** (Hebrews 1:1-3, KJV)

God as "Life" Creator and Sustainer controls every aspect of life on earth. It is He who determines who and what lives or dies. All things are in His command.

For the believer, there is a double blessing. Not only have we been given the opportunity of living here on earth, but we have the certain assurance that when Christ (in whom is rooted our eternal life) shall appear, we shall appear with Him. No wonder Paul encourages us to "set our affections on things above, not on things on earth."

> **"If ye then be risen with Christ, seek those things which are above, where Christ sitteth on the right hand of God. <u>Set your affection on things above, not on things on the earth</u>. For ye are dead, and <u>your life is hid with Christ in God</u>. When <u>Christ, who is our life</u>, shall appear, then shall ye also appear with him in glory."** (Colossians 3:1-4, KJV)

What an outstanding privilege we have of speaking directly to God, here and now, through the action of our High Priest, Jesus Christ. We are encouraged to approach God at any time and in any circumstance. He has the power to create and sustain life. He is conscious of our individual needs at all times and has the authority and ability to take action in any situation that we may face as individuals:

> **"Let us therefore come boldly unto the throne of grace, that we may obtain mercy, and find grace to <u>help in time of need</u>."** (Hebrews 4:16, KJV)

THE LIGHT

> **"This then is the message which we have heard of him, and declare unto you, that <u>God is light</u>, and in him is no darkness at all."** (1 John 1:5, KJV)

Light 1 John 1:5 <u>Definition</u>: (1) A form of energy that provides information to the brain; hence, knowledge. (2) A form of energy that stimulates and sustains life. (3) Also a form of energy which can be converted into any other expressions of energy such as light into electricity and electricity into magnetic force. In modern science, matter and energy are regarded as equivalents, mutually convertible according to Einstein's formula (energy equals mass multiplied by the square of the velocity of light).

There are three definitions of light that we are going to consider as stated in the paragraph above. All are fascinating as applied to the person of God and what we can learn about Him. We will ponder each of them separately.

Definition: We are told that He is light. (1) Light is the energy or force that brings knowledge and understanding. It is the means by which information is transmitted to living beings through the senses that are available to them. In the case of human beings, it is to *see, hear, taste, touch* and *smell.*

For instance, we can learn that something is rotten by smelling it or touching it or tasting it or seeing it. But in all cases, there is a force, energy, dynamism that conveys the information to the brain. Once the information is transmitted, the individual can take whatever action is deemed appropriate. That energy gives us the power of enlightenment. It is the light that banishes darkness or ignorance.

When any of the five senses are compromised, the light of knowledge takes another route. For example, if a person becomes blind the other senses become more critical and active. Enlightenment travels by sound, hearing, and touch, i.e., a blind man learns to read by using braille. The force enters his brain through the sense of touch. He is enlightened by the information conveyed.

Helen Keller became renowned as an example of one who was shut out of the world around her by the loss of her two major senses (sight and hearing) as an infant. Yet through the wisdom, discipline, and patience of others, she was enlightened through her other senses to the point where she was able to earn a university degree. The light of God penetrated the darkness.

This line of reasoning can be applied to animals and other creatures. The energy of enlightenment is always available to them to be used in a learning process to the maximum of their capacity, to absorb information through the senses that have been given to them.

The psalmist learned to use the word of God to become enlightened as he gained knowledge for the direction he should travel, as he treads the pathway of life.

> **"Thy word is a lamp unto my feet, and a light unto my path."** (Psalm 119:105, KJV)

The apostle John tells us that the Word (Jesus Christ) enlightens every man that comes into the world:

> **"There was a man sent from God, whose name was John. The same came for a witness, to bear witness of the Light that all men through him might believe. He was not that Light, but was sent to bear witness of that Light. <u>That was the true Light, which lighteth every man that cometh into the world</u>."** (John 1:6-9, KJV)

<u>Definition (2)</u>:

Light is a form of energy that stimulates and sustains life. Experience, simple observation, and common sense indicate that if light is withheld from vegetation, it eventually dies. If there were no vegetation to eat, there would be no animal vegetarians; thus, there would be no animals for carnivores to eat. Since there would be no animals or vegetables to eat, life on earth (as we know it) including mankind, would cease to exist.

The constant stream of light from God maintains all the forms of life with which we are surrounded and which we take for granted every day.

We remind ourselves again of the words in Hebrews, "<u>He upholds all things by the word of His power</u>":

> **"God, who at sundry times and in divers manners spake in time past unto the fathers by the prophets, Hath in these last days spoken unto us by his Son, whom he hath appointed heir of all things, by whom also he made the worlds; Who being the brightness of his glory, and the express image of his person, <u>and upholding all things by the word of his power,</u>**

when he had by himself purged our sins, sat down on the right hand of the Majesty on high." (Hebrews 1:1-3, KJV)

Definition (3):

Light is also a form of energy which can be converted into any other expressions of energy, such as light into electricity and electricity into magnetic force. In modern science, matter and energy are regarded as equivalents, mutually convertible according to Einstein's formula (energy equals mass multiplied by the square of the velocity of light).

I do not have the scientific training or education to speak with personal authority on this definition of light. However, the conclusion that scientists have arrive at over the past few generations is that all matter is composed of atoms. And atoms are made up of various combinations of energy. Each individual energy formula will determine whether the object will be steel or wood or rocks or water or whatever type of matter. This information is public knowledge, and the application of it as it relates to the person of God is revealing.

Therefore, a wooden rocking chair or a lump of coal or a tomato are all composed of tiny units of energy held in place to appear to be a solid object. Each of them can be broken down (given the right circumstances) into active forms of energy.

Consider a simple illustration. The wooden chair can be broken into pieces and set on fire. A container of water can be placed on top of the fire, and the energy from the burning wood will be transferred from the wood by heat. The energy absorbed by the water will become steam. The steam can be captured and converted into electricity by a generator. The electricity can be transported to an incandescent light bulb, and the bulb will produce light . . . and on and on and on.

Probably, the most outstanding contemporary example is the releasing of atomic power in uranium that can provide energy for large segments of societies to light and heat their homes, cook their food, and sundry other applications.

Investigative science tells us that there are 105 different chemical elements from which all material substances are constructed. The differing factor is the amount of atomic energy found in each element. No two elements have the same atomic makeup.

How and where did it all begin?

Could the first chapter of Genesis provide some clues?

Verse one makes the flat statement that God created the heaven and the earth. There are no details to that point.

> **"In the beginning God created the heaven and the earth."**
> (Genesis 1:1, KJV)

Were all the 105 elements mentioned above made available at that moment, as building blocks for the universe? Was it because they were not yet organized into material substance, the reason that everything appeared to be without form and void until the Spirit of God took action?

> **"And the earth was without form, and void; and darkness was upon the face of the deep. <u>And the Spirit of God moved upon the face of the waters</u>."** (Genesis 1:2, KJV)

And is it any wonder that God as Light would enter the scene and organize the chaos?

> **"And God said, <u>Let there be light: and there was light</u>. And God saw the light, that it was good: and God divided the light from the darkness. And God called the light Day, and the darkness he called Night. And the evening and the morning were the first day."** (Genesis 1:3-5, KJV)

It seems that God caused a separation or firmament to occur between the material (waters) around the earth and the material (waters) in the heavens.

> **"And God said, Let there be a firmament in the midst of the waters, and let it divide the waters from the waters. And <u>God</u>**

made the firmament, and divided the waters which were under the firmament from the waters which were above the firmament: and it was so. And God called the firmament Heaven. And the evening and the morning were the second day." (Genesis 1:6-8, KJV)

The sequence of the creation of light, followed by the organization of the earth and sky and coupled with the connection of light and mass (in Einstein's theory), could lead one to think that energy as light emanating from the person of God played a major part in the establishment of all the material things that form the earth and the universe.

"And God said, Let the waters under the heaven be gathered together unto one place, and let the dry land appear: and it was so. And God called the dry land Earth; and the gathering together of the waters called He Seas: and God saw that it was good." (Genesis 1:9-10, KJV)

The stage was set for the establishment of life on earth: vegetation, then fish, fowl, and animals, and, finally, mankind.

"And God said, Let the earth bring forth grass, the herb yielding seed, and the fruit tree yielding fruit after his kind, whose seed is in itself, upon the earth: and it was so." (Genesis 1:11, KJV)

God as *Light* leaves us with such a vista of images that it is extremely difficult to find the words to summarize in any meaningful fashion the impact He has on everything, every moment. He causes information to flow constantly to living creatures He has created. He controls the dissemination of knowledge and thereby dissipates darkness and ignorance. The psalmist states the case most eloquently:

"The heavens declare the glory of God; and the firmament sheweth his handywork. Day unto day uttereth speech, and night unto night sheweth knowledge. There is no speech nor language, where their voice is not heard. Their line is gone out through all the earth, and their words to the end of the world. In them hath he set a tabernacle for the sun, which is

as a bridegroom coming out of his chamber, and rejoiceth as a strong man to run a race. <u>His going forth is from the end of the heaven, and his circuit unto the ends of it: and there is nothing hid from the heat thereof.</u>" (Psalm 19:1-6, KJV)

He constantly mixes, moves, and combines the 105 chemical elements He fashioned into useful things . . . things such as combining hydrogen and oxygen (H2O) into water that becomes distributed throughout the world, providing a major ingredient for the sustenance of all life.

"Sing unto the LORD with thanksgiving; sing praise upon the harp unto our God: Who covereth the heaven with clouds, <u>who prepareth rain for the earth</u>, who maketh grass to grow upon the mountains. He giveth to the beast his food, and to the young ravens which cry." (Psalm 147:7-9, KJV)

If that were not enough, the Lord Jesus promised to provide the light of life to all that believe in Him. This sweeps away the ignorance, doubt, and darkness surrounding our eternal welfare.

"Then spake Jesus again unto them, saying, <u>I am the light of the world: he that followeth me shall not walk in darkness, but shall have the light of life</u>." (John 8:12, KJV)

"For God, who commanded the light to shine out of darkness, hath shined in our hearts, <u>to give the light of the knowledge of the glory of God in the face of Jesus Christ</u>." (2 Corinthians 4:6, KJV)

In the end, the redeemed shall live in the light of His presence, without any longer the temporary employment of the sun, etc.

"And there shall be no more curse: but the throne of God and of the Lamb shall be in it; and his servants shall serve him: And they shall see his face; and his name shall be in their foreheads. And <u>there shall be no night there; and they need no candle, neither light of the sun; for the Lord God giveth them light</u>: and they shall reign for ever and ever." (Revelation 22:3-5, KJV)

LOVE

"And we have known and believed the love that God hath to us. <u>God is love</u>; and he that dwelleth in love dwelleth in God, and God in him!" (John 4:16, KJV)

<u>Definition</u>: Love is the emotional force that creates and sustains social relationships between living beings.

God released the powerful force of love from His person to inundate the animals on earth, to be used by them to accomplish and retain interaction and social relationships among themselves. And in the case of human beings, to respond to the love of God directed toward them.

Jesus said:

> **Thou shalt <u>love the Lord thy God</u> with all thy heart, and with all thy soul, and with all thy strength, and with all thy mind; and <u>thy neighbour as thyself</u>."** (Luke 10:27, KJV)

Hate is the same emotional force as love. There is a point at which love becomes hate. There are different degrees of intensity between passionate love and passionate hate. To illustrate:

> **LOVE** . . . like . . . tolerate . . . dislike . . . **HATE**

This contrast used in the juxtaposition of the description of the attitude of the Son of God toward good and evil implies the same force is in play.

> **"Thou hast <u>loved righteousness</u>, and <u>hated iniquity</u>; therefore God, even thy God, hath anointed thee with the oil of gladness above thy fellows."** (Hebrews 1:9, KJV)

The words of Jesus, as He assesses the state of the seven churches in their relationship with Him, distinguish a middle area between love and hate. He deems them to be "neither hot nor cold, but lukewarm."

"So then because thou art <u>lukewarm,</u> and neither cold nor hot, I will spue thee out of my mouth." (Revelation 3:16, KJV)

Every other emotion experienced by humanity and other animals has its roots in this *love* or *hate* force that has been unleashed by the Creator.

In this segment, we will emphasize the passionate love of God. His passionate hate we will consider later.

Passionate love demands to be expressed.

When one has a passionate love for another person or one's country or a sports team, etc., there is a compulsive need to vent that feeling.

Jesus explained it this way:

"A good man out of the good treasure of his heart bringeth forth that which is good; and an evil man out of the evil treasure of his heart bringeth forth that which is evil: for <u>of the abundance of the heart his mouth speaketh</u>." (Luke 6:45, KJV)

There are two major ways to express passionate love: (1) by giving presents, and (2) by giving one's presence.

When we watch the behavior of humans "in love," we find that they try to find presents for the object of their affections (flowers, jewelry, special dinner, etc.).

When we see God expressing His love for humanity, we are overwhelmed by the magnitude and variety of His presents (flowers, animals, trees, beauty, music, food, etc.), and the senses to enjoy it all.

Humans, when they express this God-given passionate love, strive to be with each other as much as possible to share time, energy, service, and companionship.

From the very beginning, God has demonstrated His passionate love by wanting to share companionship with mankind. He has continued that pursuit to this day. His greatest present and His greatest presence is the gift of His Son:

> "<u>This is how God showed his love</u> among us: He sent his one and only Son into the world that we might live through him. This is love: not that we loved God, but that he loved us and <u>sent his Son as an atoning sacrifice for our sins</u>." (1 John 3:9-10, NIV)

God continues that outpouring of His love today through the gift of the companionship of the Holy Spirit as promised by Jesus:

> "I have yet many things to say unto you, but ye cannot bear them now. Howbeit when he, the Spirit of truth, is come, he will guide you into all truth: for he shall not speak of himself; but whatsoever he shall hear, that shall he speak: and he will shew you things to come. <u>He shall glorify me: for he shall receive of mine, and shall shew it unto you</u>." (John 16:12-14, KJV)

This rapport He will sustain throughout eternity:

> "And I heard a great voice out of heaven saying, Behold, <u>the tabernacle of God is with men, and he will dwell with them, and they shall be his people, and God himself shall be with them, and be their God.</u> And God shall wipe away all tears from their eyes; and there shall be no more death, neither sorrow, nor crying, neither shall there be any more pain: for the former things are passed away." (Revelation 21:2-3, KJV)

God painted a clear graphic portrait of the extent of His love to Israel through the life of Hosea. He wanted this prophet to live a life that would bring into the glare of daylight the horribleness of the actions of the nation throughout every generation. They repeatedly turned away from the loving care of God to fill their devotion with the idols of the nations around them instead of casting them off forever. He again and again placed His loving arms around them and gave them another chance, despite the fact that they continually chose prostitution instead of a loving companionship with Him

> **"And the LORD said to Hosea, Go, take unto thee a wife of whoredoms and children of whoredoms: for the land hath committed great whoredom, departing from the LORD."** (Hosea 1:2, KJV)

Before His sacrificial death on the cross, the Lord Jesus, expressing His passionate love for Israel, spoke these words:

> **"O Jerusalem, Jerusalem, thou that killest the prophets, and stonest them which are sent unto thee, <u>how often would I have gathered thy children together, even as a hen gathereth her chickens under her wings, and ye would not!</u> Behold, your house is left unto you desolate. For I say unto you, Ye shall not see me henceforth, till ye shall say, Blessed is he that cometh in the name of the Lord."** (Matthew 23:37-39, KJV)

God's relationship with the Nation of Israel is mirrored by His experience with mankind in general.

The apostle Paul in his description of the depravity of humanity included these words:

> **"Who changed the truth of God into a lie, and <u>worshipped and served the creature more than the Creator</u>."** (Romans 1:25, KJV)

In the face of all that, God still loves us and demonstrated His love as told by John:

> **"This is how God showed his love among us: He sent his one and only Son into the world that we might live through him. <u>This is love: not that we loved God, but that he loved us and sent his Son as an atoning sacrifice for our sins</u>."** (1 John 4:9-10, KJV)

To love is to risk. Great joy or great sorrow can result from the expression of love. It depends on the response of the object loved.

Jesus Christ took the greatest possible risk in giving Himself to a humanity of prostitutes from the beginning of time (to use the Hosea example). His desire is to take them into His own dwelling and lavish upon them the gift of His love. Some have responded and accepted Him. Others have squandered their love on the false gods society has to offer . . . and have rejected Him.

> **"I say unto you, that likewise <u>joy shall be in heaven over one sinner</u> that repenteth, more than over ninety and nine just persons, which need no repentance."** (Luke 15:7, KJV)

We learn from these few thoughts that God loves human beings so much that He is in constant pursuit of them and has emptied the treasure of heaven to win their love. Let us appropriate Paul's prayer and apply it to ourselves:

> **"That Christ may dwell in your hearts by faith; that ye, being rooted and grounded in love, [18] May be able to comprehend with all saints what is the breadth, and length, and depth, and height; [19] And <u>to know the love of Christ, which passeth knowledge, that ye might be filled with all the fulness of God</u>."** (Ephesians 3:17-19, KJV)

The Beginning and the End

> **"And he said unto me, It is done. <u>I am Alpha and Omega, the beginning and the end.</u> I will give unto him that is athirst of the fountain of the water of life freely."** (Revelation 21:6, KJV)

<u>Definition</u>: Eternity

To have some concept of eternity, one should first consider the perception of time.

We usually associate the passing of time with how long people have lived. Today, the thought of a person living for one hundred years or more attracts attention. Six or seven thousand years ago, it was not unusual to live eight hundred to nine hundred years. Methusalah lived to be 969 years old according to the Bible. About three thousand years ago, the psalmist estimated that the life span of a person was sixty or seventy years, eighty years max:

> "We spend our years as a tale that is told. <u>The days of our years are threescore years and ten;</u> and if by reason of strength they be fourscore years, yet is their strength labour and sorrow; for it is soon cut off, and we fly away." (Psalm 90:9-10, KJV)

We probably would agree with the description Peter gives when he wrote to the Christians in the days of the early church:

> "For all flesh is as grass, and all the glory of man as the flower of grass. The grass withereth, and the flower thereof falleth away!" (Peter 1:24, KJV)

Compared to the estimated age of the earth, man's presence on the globe is miniscule. According to Wikipedia, the age of the Earth (based on radiometric dating) is 4.54 billion years. When we extend our thought process to consider the galaxy in which we live, the time or space numbers start to become overwhelming.

In order to maintain some degree of perspective, we need to keep in mind that the speed of light is 186,282 miles *per second*. A "light-year'" is the number of miles a beam of light would travel in a year at the rate of 186,282 miles per second. [186,282 X (the number of seconds in a year)]. It is the mental graphic connecting point to help us grasp the enormity of the subject matter that follows. With the intention of getting an appreciation of the measurement of time, we need to assume that time began at the precise moment of the creation of the universe. By measuring the distance between some of the ingredients of the universe, we can begin to assimilate the vast scope of time.

Our galaxy, the Milky Way, is a *spiral galaxy* of one hundred thousand light-years in diameter containing two hundred to four hundred billion stars. Our sun is one of them.

Our neighboring galaxy, Andromeda, is estimated to have one trillion stars and fifty billion planets.

There are probably more than 170 billion galaxies in the observable universe.

The diameter of the observable universe is estimated to be about ninety-three billion light-years, putting the edge of the observable universe at about forty-six to forty-seven billion light-years away. The universe has been rapidly expanding since creation.

The age of the universe is about 13.75 billion years. The extent of time past is staggering and breaches the limited boundaries of the imagination of the human mind.

According to the verse at the opening of this section of our contemplation, God *is* the beginning and therefore was present before the beginning, and therefore, He *is* eternity past.

What about the end of time in the future? When and how will it be?

This was the question that the disciples asked Jesus, when this subject arose out of their conversation:

> **"And as he sat upon the mount of Olives, the disciples came unto him privately, saying, Tell us, when shall these things be? and <u>what shall be the sign of thy coming, and of the end of the world</u>?"** (Matthew 24:3, KJ)

Jesus outlined many things that would precede His return. One of them is the convulsion of the heavens:

> **"Immediately after the tribulation of those days shall the sun be darkened, and the moon shall not give her light, and <u>the</u>**

stars shall fall from heaven, and the powers of the heavens shall be shaken:" (Matthew 24:29, KJV)

Jesus said that the heavens and earth will definitely pass away, but no one but God the Father knows the exact time.

"Heaven and earth shall pass away, but my words shall not pass away. But of that day and hour knoweth no man, no, not the angels of heaven, but my Father only" (Matthew 24:25, KJV)

Peter gives us a vivid account of the striking aftermath of the coming of the Lord:

"But the day of the Lord will come as a thief in the night; in the which the heavens shall pass away with a great noise, and the elements shall melt with fervent heat, the earth also and the works that are therein shall be burned up." (2 Peter 3:10, KJV)

Peter continues to encourage present-day believers to enliven their daily behavior in the light of these coming events and not to invest their demeanor in the current passing of time because it will all end.

"Seeing then that all these things shall be dissolved, what manner of persons ought ye to be in all holy conversation and godliness, [12] Looking for and hasting unto the coming of the day of God, wherein the heavens being on fire shall be dissolved, and the elements shall melt with fervent heat?" (2 Peter 3:11-12, KJV)

The contemporary disciple is spurred on by the thought that God has promised a new heaven and a new earth to begin the future eternity.

"Nevertheless we, according to his promise, look for new heavens and a new earth, wherein dwelleth righteousness." (2 Peter 3:13, KJV)

As promised, the age and time will be done, finished, over, as described in Revelation 21:

> "And I saw a <u>new heaven and a new earth</u>: for the <u>first heaven and the first earth were passed away</u> . . . And he that sitteth on the throne said, Behold, <u>I make all things new</u>. And he saith, Write: for these words are faithful and true. ⁶ And he said unto me, <u>They are come to pass</u>. <u>I am the Alpha and the Omega, the beginning and the end</u>." (KJV)

In the midst of the grandeur, splendor, and majesty of being the Creator and Sustainer of the universe, He is still obsessed with His relationship with the individual human being.

> "Thus saith the LORD, The heaven is my throne, and the earth is my footstool: where is the house that ye build unto me? and where is the place of my rest? For all those things hath mine hand made, and all those things have been, saith the LORD: but <u>to this man will I look</u>, even to him that is <u>poor</u> and of a <u>contrite spirit</u>, and <u>trembleth at my word</u>." (Isaiah 66:1-2, KJV)

The discussion as to Biblical creation dates and scientific finding is irrelevant when we consider the following:

> "But, beloved, be not ignorant of this one thing, that <u>one day</u> is <u>with the Lord as a thousand years</u>, and <u>a thousand years as one day</u>." (2 Peter 3:8, KJV)

> "For a <u>thousand years in thy sight are but as yesterday when it is past, and as a watch in the night</u>." (Psalm 90:4, KJV)

> "For <u>my thoughts are not your thoughts, neither are your ways my ways</u>, saith Jehovah. For as the heavens are higher than the earth, so are my ways higher than your ways, and my thoughts than your thoughts." (Isaiah 55:8-9, KJV)

> "Hast thou not known? hast thou not heard, that the everlasting God, the LORD, the Creator of the ends of the

earth, fainteth not, neither is weary? <u>There is no searching of his understanding.</u>" (Isaiah 40:28, KJV)

As humans, we are mentally ambushed by the raw power, the gentleness, the majesty of our God as demonstrated by all His handiwork on every side. Surely, we can join together with the psalmist when he said,

> "**When I consider thy heavens, the work of thy fingers, the moon and the stars, which thou hast ordained; <u>What is man, that thou art mindful of him? and the son of man, that thou visitest him?</u> For thou hast made him a little lower than the angels, and hast crowned him with glory and honour. Thou madest him to have dominion over the works of thy hands; thou hast put all things under his feet: All sheep and oxen, yea, and the beasts of the field; The fowl of the air, and the fish of the sea, and whatsoever passeth through the paths of the seas. <u>O LORD our Lord, how excellent is thy name in all the earth!</u>**" (Psalm 8:3-9, KJV)

<u>Consuming Fire</u>

> "**Wherefore we receiving a kingdom which cannot be moved, let us have grace, whereby we may serve God acceptably with reverence and godly fear: <u>For our God is a consuming fire.</u>**" (Heb. 12:28-29, KJV)

<u>Definition</u>: The final Judge

God is going to remove every vestige of sin from His universe. All things were made for His glory, and anything that is left standing by the end of time, that does not meet this standard, will be stripped away, will be exterminated, obliterated, put into the place of death, and separated from Him for eternity. This applies to the highest spirit being, to the lowest human being.

This is forcefully expressed in the message paraphrase of the scripture:

"Do you see what we've got? An unshakable kingdom! And do you see how thankful we must be? Not only thankful, but brimming with worship, deeply reverent before God. For God is not an indifferent bystander. He's actively cleaning house, torching all that needs to burn, and he won't quit until it's all cleansed. God himself is Fire!" (Hebrews 12:28-29, the Message)

God has created every being for His glory. The assessment that the apostle Paul made as he evaluated the condition of humanity on this subject was that "all have sinned and fallen short of the glory of God."

"For all have sinned, and come short of the glory of God." (Romans 3:23, KJV)

Man was created in the image of God. To achieve that quality for humans is still the intent of God. That was His purpose at the beginning. His purpose will ultimately be fulfilled.

"According as he hath chosen us in him before the foundation of the world, that we should be holy and without blame before him in love: Having predestinated us unto the adoption of children by Jesus Christ to himself, according to the good pleasure of his will," (Ephesians 1:4-5, KJV)

This strict judgment applies to the works of those who have been born into His family, first and foremost, so that they may be made fit for his presence.

"Every man's work shall be made manifest: for the day shall declare it, because it shall be revealed by fire; and the fire shall try every man's work of what sort it is. If any man's work abide which he hath built thereupon, he shall receive a reward. If any man's work shall be burned, he shall suffer loss: but he himself shall be saved; yet so as by fire." (1 Corinthians 3:13-17, KJV)

It is often said that the "God of the New Testament" is different from the "God of the Old Testament." It is true that we are not under the law as the

Israelites were but under grace. However, it is the same God who is dealing with the fulfilling of His decrees. We are trying to grasp what God is like; therefore, we must face this fact and review some of the incidents that demonstrate this characteristic of God.

We have spent some time meditating on the love of God. We must also think about the other end of the force of love which is hate. To repeat again, the scripture in Hebrews that tells us what God hates and the reaction He has.

> **"But unto the Son he saith, Thy throne, O God, is for ever and ever: a sceptre of righteousness is the sceptre of thy kingdom. Thou hast loved righteousness, and <u>hated iniquity</u>;"** (Hebrews 1:7-9, KJV)

It was not long after sin entered the human race, through the fall of Adam and Eve, that the entire population of the earth became putrid. The stench rose to heaven. God hated the iniquitous behavior. He decided to wipe out all animal life on the planet, with the exception of Noah and his family who found grace in His eyes, plus the animals he collected in the ark:

> **"And GOD saw that <u>the wickedness of man was great in the earth, and that every imagination of the thoughts of his heart was only evil continually</u>. And it repented the LORD that he had made man on the earth, and <u>it grieved him at his heart</u>. And the LORD said, <u>I will destroy man whom I have created from the face of the earth</u>; both man, and beast, and the creeping thing, and the fowls of the air; for it repenteth me that I have made them."** (Genesis 6:5-7, KJV)

> **"<u>And all flesh died that moved upon the earth</u>, both of fowl, and of cattle, and of beast, and of every creeping thing that creepeth upon the earth, and <u>every man</u>: All in whose nostrils was the breath of life, of all that was in the dry land, died. And <u>every living substance was destroyed</u> which was upon the face of the ground, both man, and cattle, and the creeping things, and the fowl of the heaven; and <u>they were destroyed from the earth</u>:"** (Genesis 7:21-23)

Through Noah and his family, the earth was repopulated.

Subsequently, God selected one man, Abraham, through whom he promised to make a nation. Eventually, that nation was named "Israel." Through a variety of circumstances, Israel found itself in captivity in Egypt but was miraculously rescued by the direct hand of God.

God made it perfectly clear to the Israelites what He considered to be "iniquity" when He gave them the Ten Commandments. At the head of the list was the prohibition of putting anything or anyone else ahead of Him in the worship and affections of the human heart.

> **"And God spake all these words, saying, <u>I am the LORD thy God</u>, which have brought thee out of the land of Egypt, out of the house of bondage. <u>Thou shalt have no other gods before me.</u> Thou shalt not make unto thee any graven image, or any likeness of anything that is in heaven above, or that is in the earth beneath, or that is in the water under the earth: <u>Thou shalt not bow down thyself to them, nor serve them:</u> <u>for I the LORD thy God am a jealous God</u>,"** (Exodus 20:1-5)

Even while Moses was receiving these orders from God, the Israelites erected a metal calf and were worshipping it. They were also engaging in monstrous sexual activities, in contrast to the specific directives from God. He ordered an immediate response by having three thousand people slaughtered by sword, to express His hatred of their iniquity.

> **"Then Moses stood in the gate of the camp, and said, 'Who is on the LORD'S side?,' let him come unto me. And all the sons of Levi gathered themselves together unto him. [27] And he said unto them, <u>Thus saith the LORD God of Israel</u>, 'Put every man his sword by his side, and go in and out from gate to gate throughout the camp, and <u>slay every man his brother, and every man his companion, and every man his neighbour.</u>' And the children of Levi did according to the word of Moses: <u>and there fell of the people that day about three thousand men</u>."** (Exodus 32:26-28)

During the succeeding history of Israel, there were many instances where the wrath of God against iniquity of one kind and another were met with the relentless execution of the fury of God. One of them was the case of Korah. He and some of his associates were jealous of the position of authority that God had placed upon Moses and Aaron. Korah stirred up the entire nation and challenged Moses. Moses brought the matter to God. The result was the destruction of Korah, his confederates, their families, possessions—everything associated with him. They were swallowed up by the earth . . . men, women, children, and property. Moses told the rest of the nation to stand back from Korah and his associates so they would not be destroyed with them:

> "And <u>the earth opened her mouth, and swallowed them up,</u> <u>and their houses, and all the men that appertained unto</u> <u>Korah, and all their goods. They, and all that appertained to</u> <u>them, went down alive into the pit, and the earth closed upon</u> <u>them: and they perished from among the congregation.</u>" (Numbers 16:32-33, KJV)

Throughout their history, the Israelites repeatedly turned to idolatry. God over and over again chastised them directly or through the armies of their enemies, slaughtering thousands upon thousands of men, women, and children. One of those occasions is described by the psalmist:

> "For <u>they provoked him to anger with their high places, and</u> <u>moved him to jealousy with their graven images. When God</u> <u>heard this, he was wroth, and greatly abhorred Israel:</u> So that he forsook the tabernacle of Shiloh, the tent which he placed among men; And delivered his strength into captivity, and his glory into the enemy's hand. <u>He gave his people over also</u> <u>unto the sword;</u> and was wroth with his inheritance. <u>The</u> <u>fire consumed their young men;</u> and their maidens were not given to marriage. <u>Their priests fell by the sword;</u> and their widows made no lamentation." (Psalm 78:57-64, KJV)

The character of God does not change from one generation to another or from one millennium to another. He remains unswerving and unassailable. The writer to the Hebrews said,

"And, Thou, Lord, in the beginning hast laid the foundation of the earth; and the heavens are the works of thine hands: They shall perish; but <u>thou remainest</u>; and they all shall wax old as doth a garment; And as a vesture shalt thou fold them up, and they shall be changed: but <u>thou art the same</u>, and <u>thy years shall not fail.</u>" (Hebrews 1:10-12, KJV)

"Jesus Christ <u>the same yesterday, and today, and forever.</u>" (Hebrews 13:8, KJV)

He is the same person as He was when He wiped out the entire population of the earth in the great flood. He is the same person as He was when He caused the Israelites to be slaughtered by the thousands because of their idolatry. He is the same person that will be on the throne to judge and to condemn Satan and his angels for exalting themselves above God and cast them into the lake of fire.

"And there was war in heaven: Michael and his angels fought against the dragon; and the dragon fought and his angels, And prevailed not; neither was their place found any more in heaven. And <u>the great dragon was cast out, that old serpent, called the Devil, and Satan,</u> which deceiveth the whole world: <u>he was cast out into the earth, and his angels were cast out with him.</u>" (Revelation 12:7-10, KJV)

"<u>God spared not the angels that sinned, but cast them down to hell,</u> and delivered them into chains of darkness, to be <u>reserved unto judgment;</u>" (2 Peter 2:4-5)

"And <u>the devil that deceived them was cast into the lake of fire and brimstone,</u> where the beast and the false prophet are, and shall be tormented day and night for ever and ever" (Revelation 20:11)

He is the same person who will occupy the great white throne before whom all the humans whose names are not written in the Book of Life will be deemed to have rejected Him. They will fall short of His glory and therefore will be cut off from Him, who is life. They will endure His fiery judgment.

"I saw a great white throne and Him that sat on it, from whose face the earth and the heaven fled away; and there was found no place for them. And I saw the dead, small and great, stand before God; and the books were opened: and another book was opened, which is the book of life: and the dead were judged out of those things which were written in the books, according to their Works. And the sea gave up the dead which were in it; and death and hell delivered up the dead which were in them: and they were judged every man according to their works. And death and hell were cast into the lake of fire. This is the second death And whosoever was not found written in the book of life was cast into the lake of fire." (Revelation 20:11-15, KJV)

Every vestige, trace, hint, source, cause, outcome, and end result of sin, iniquity, and anything falling short of the glory of God will have been eradicated, obliterated, erased, demolished, and destroyed. God will make all things new, and there will only be found peace, health, and vitality. There will be no chance for the disease of sin to spread again because it will have been completely blotted out . . . purified by the blood of Christ.

"And I saw no temple therein: for the Lord God Almighty and the Lamb are the temple of it. And the city had no need of the sun, neither of the moon, to shine in it: for the glory of God did lighten it, and the Lamb is the light thereof. And the nations of them which are saved shall walk in the light of it: and the kings of the earth do bring their glory and honour into it. And the gates of it shall not be shut at all by day: for there shall be no night there. And they shall bring the glory and honour of the nations into it. And there shall in no wise enter into it anything that defileth, neither whatsoever worketh abomination, or maketh a lie: but they which are written in the Lamb's book of life." (Revelation 21:22-27, KJV)

"And when all things shall be subdued unto him, then shall the Son also himself be subject unto him that put all things under him, that God may be all in all." (1 Corinthians 15:28)

"Eye hath not seen, nor ear heard, neither have entered into the heart of man, the things which God hath prepared for them that love him. But God hath revealed them unto us by his Spirit: for the Spirit searcheth all things, yea, the deep things of God" (1 Corinthians 2:9-10)

Chapter 7

God Is Spirit

HE LEFT AT dawn to walk to the next place He intended to visit. He was accompanied by a few friends. By noon, they reached a well near a village. It had been a hot, dry traipse, and He was thirsty and felt the need to rest. His companions left Him beside the well and proceeded into the town to get some supplies.

She was up at dawn and, as usual, watched the other women in the village gather together and make their way to the nearby well to get their supply of water for the day, before the sweltering heat made the unpleasant task all the more onerous.

Years ago, she had found her place among them every day at this time; but now she was unwelcomed, spurned, and disparaged. She had become virtually an outcast among the girls with whom she had socialized since childhood. The events of life had not been kind to her. For one reason or another, she had lost five husbands, and she had now taken habitation with a man who was not her husband. This litany of experiences enflamed her friends to turn against her, using sharp-cutting words to purposefully hurt her already-raw feelings. Consequently, she avoided going to the well when all the rest of the women did. She waited until the heat of the day, at noon, when no one would be there to taunt her. She had taken precaution to carry out her task so that she would not encounter other people, and here, someone was in the space at the well that she had hoped to have reserved for herself. He was a stranger, and by his garb, she suspected that he was a Jew. He spoke to her, and then by his accent, she knew he was a Jew. She was a Samaritan.

The Jews despised the Samaritans because of past political, social, and religious differences, even though both clans shared the same genealogy at their beginning. The Jews considered the Samaritans crossbreeds and would not associate or speak to them, if at all possible. She was not going to allow him to demean her and decided to go on the attack.

She gave him a sardonic verbal chiding for speaking to a Samaritan . . . and a woman Samaritan at that.

He thwarted the rudeness of her cutting remarks by asking a question that exposed the blackened bruises of the battering from the events of her life. This short revelation took her breath away. She was ready to listen to anything He had to say . . . and He had plenty to say!

He was Jesus, the Creator of the universe and everything that is in it.

She was an unnamed, broken Samaritan woman who was even vilified by the villagers where she lived. She was an unlikely recipient of the outstanding, astounding information He was about to tell her:

o   He offered her living water that would sustain her through time and eternity.

o   He told her that God is spirit.

o   He told her that God must be worshiped in reality.

o   That the act of worshiping God is not limited to specific buildings or localities on earth, but through the Spirit anywhere.

o   She was one of the few people He directly told that He was the Messiah.

> **"When therefore the Lord knew how the Pharisees had heard that Jesus made and baptized more disciples than John, (Though Jesus himself baptized not, but his disciples,) He left Judaea, and departed again into Galilee <u>he must needs go through Samaria.</u> Then cometh he to a city of Samaria, which is called Sychar, near to the parcel of ground that Jacob gave to his son Joseph. Now Jacob's well was there. Jesus therefore, being wearied with his journey, sat thus on the well: and it was about the sixth hour. There cometh a**

woman of Samaria to draw water: Jesus saith unto her, Give me to drink. (For his disciples were gone away unto the city to buy meat.) Then saith the woman of Samaria unto him, how is it that thou, being a Jew, askest drink of me, which am a woman of Samaria? For the Jews have no dealings with the Samaritans. Jesus answered and said unto her, If thou knewest the gift of God, and who it is that saith to thee, Give me to drink; thou wouldest have asked of him, and he would have given thee living water. The woman saith unto him, Sir, thou hast nothing to draw with, and the well is deep: from whence then hast thou that living water? Art thou greater than our father Jacob, which gave us the well, and drank thereof himself, and his children, and his cattle? Jesus answered and said unto her, Whosoever drinketh of this water shall thirst again: But whosoever drinketh of the water that I shall give him shall never thirst; but the water that I shall give him shall be in him a well of water springing up into everlasting life. The woman saith unto him, Sir, give me this water, that I thirst not, neither come hither to draw. Jesus saith unto her, Go, call thy husband, and come hither. The woman answered and said, I have no husband. Jesus said unto her, Thou hast well said, I have no husband: For thou hast had five husbands; and he whom thou now hast is not thy husband: in that saidst thou truly. The woman saith unto him, Sir, I perceive that thou art a prophet. Our fathers worshipped in this mountain; and ye say, that in Jerusalem is the place where men ought to worship. Jesus saith unto her, Woman, believe me, the hour cometh, when ye shall neither in this mountain, nor yet at Jerusalem, worship the Father. Ye worship ye know not what: we know what we worship: for salvation is of the Jews. But the hour cometh, and now is, when the true worshippers shall worship the Father in spirit and in truth: for the Father seeketh such to worship him. God is a Spirit: and they that worship him must worship him in spirit and in truth." (John 4:1-24, AV)

This was universe-shaking information! One would think that Jesus would have wanted to share it with the religious elite in Jerusalem to get the maximum coverage among the population. But no, He chose this apparently damaged, insignificant person out of the human mainstream to accomplish His purpose. It reminds us of Paul's description of how God operates:

> "For ye see your calling, brethren, how that not many wise men after the flesh, not many mighty, not many noble, are called: But <u>God hath chosen the foolish things of the world to confound the wise; and God hath chosen the weak things of the world to confound the things which are mighty; And base things of the world, and things which are despised, hath God chosen, yea, and things which are not, to bring to nought things that are:</u> That no flesh should glory in his presence." (1 Corinthians 1:26-29, AV)

Each of the topics that Jesus discussed with this woman is of tremendous significance and worthy of detailed scrutiny. However, the main purpose of our present contemplation is to have a more intimate understanding of what God is like. Our concentration is on the truth expressed by Jesus in verses 18-24:

> "Sir, I perceive that thou art a prophet. Our fathers worshipped in this mountain; and ye say, that in Jerusalem is the place where men ought to worship. <u>Jesus saith unto her, Woman, believe me, the hour cometh, when ye shall neither in this mountain, nor yet at Jerusalem, worship the Father.</u> Ye worship ye know not what: we know what we worship: for salvation is of the Jews. <u>But the hour cometh, and now is, when the true worshippers shall worship the Father in spirit and in truth:</u> for the Father seeketh such to worship him. <u>God is a Spirit: and they that worship him must worship him in spirit and in truth</u>." (John 4:18-24, AV)

To gain some appreciation of the change in human-God and God-human communication of which Jesus spoke, we refer to some of the incidents of the past recorded in the Bible, relating to the contact between God and man.

We need to recall that there was daily fellowship between God and man and man and God in the Garden of Eden. This was shattered when man disobeyed God. Adam and Eve were dispelled from Eden.

> "**After he drove the man out**, he placed on the east side of the Garden of Eden cherubim and a **flaming sword flashing back and forth to guard the way to the tree of life**." (Genesis 3:24, NIV84)

Following Adam, there were several individual humans who were in contact with God, among them was

Enoch:

> "**When Enoch had lived 65 years, he became the father of Methuselah. And after he became the father of Methuselah, Enoch walked with God 300 years and had other sons and daughters. Altogether, Enoch lived 365 years. Enoch walked with God; then he was no more, because God took him away.**" (Genesis 5:21-24, NIV84)

Noah:

> "**This is the account of Noah. Noah was a righteous man, blameless among the people of his time, and he walked with God.**" (Genesis 6:8-10, NIV84)

Abram:

> "**The LORD appeared to Abram and said, 'To your offspring I will give this land.' So he built an altar there to the LORD, who had appeared to him.**" (Genesis 12:7, NIV84)

Isaac:

> "**That night the LORD appeared to him and said, 'I am the God of your father Abraham. Do not be afraid, for I am with you; I will bless you and will increase the number of your descendants for the sake of my servant Abraham.' Isaac built**

an altar there and called on the name of the LORD. There he pitched his tent, and there his servants dug a well." (Genesis 26:21-25, NIV84)

Jacob:

The incredible story of Jacob's sons is related:

There were twelve brothers, and they wanted to get rid of Joseph, the youngest, because he was a favorite of his father. They sold their brother Joseph into slavery, and he was carried to Egypt where he became a household slave. Then amazingly, by the hand of God and through a series of events, he rose to the top echelon of power in the land.

Because of a great famine throughout that part of the world, reluctantly, Jacob was forced to move all his family and property from the territory he currently inhabited. This was difficult and painful because where he was living, he believed, was the land promised by God to Abraham.

God contacted Jacob again to assure him that this was the right step for him at that time, and that his family would become a great nation during the time they lived in Egypt.

> "And **God spoke to Israel in a vision** at night and said, 'Jacob! Jacob!' 'Here I am,' he replied. '**I am God, the God of your father**,' he said. 'Do not be afraid to go down to Egypt, **for I will make you into a great nation there.** I will go down to Egypt with you, and **I will surely bring you back again.** And Joseph's own hand will close your eyes.'" (Genesis 46:2-4, NIV84)

> "**Then Jacob left Beersheba, and Israel's sons took their father Jacob and their children and their wives in the carts that Pharaoh had sent to transport him. They also took with** them their livestock and the possessions and they had acquired in Canaan, Jacob and all his offspring went to Egypt. He took with him to Egypt his sons and grandsons and his daughters and granddaughters **all his offspring**." (Genesis 46:5-7, NIV84)

Moses:

Moses was one of the babies born into the greatly multiplied number of Jacob's descendants. By this time, the family had become the nation that God had promised. Joseph was dead, as were all the related ruling peers that were alive in his day. The children of Israel had become slaves of Egypt. It was time for God to remove this cluster of people and deal with them as a special group with whom He would establish a relationship separate from the rest of the world.

God called Moses to be the leader of this appointed people.

> **"Now Moses was tending the flock of Jethro his father-in-law, the priest of Midian, and he led the flock to the far side of the desert and came to Horeb, the mountain of God. There the angel of the LORD appeared to him in flames of fire from within a bush. Moses saw that though the bush was on fire it did not burn up. So Moses thought, 'I will go over and see this strange sight—why the bush does not burn up.'**
>
> **When the LORD saw that he had gone over to look, <u>God called to him from within the bush, 'Moses! Moses!'</u>**
>
> **And Moses said, 'Here I am.'**
>
> **<u>'Do not come any closer,' God said. 'Take off your sandals, for the place where you are standing is holy ground</u>.' Then he said, '<u>I am the God of your father, the God of Abraham, the God of Isaac and the God of Jacob.</u>' At this, Moses hid his face, because he was afraid to look at God."** (Exodus 3:1-6, NIV84)

The list of people mentioned above is composed of individuals who were sought out by God for specific purposes. From the many humans available over the time period covered, the percentage of those selected is very small. In each case, it was God who was the initiator of the contact.

It is a touching thought to realize that after the debacle with Adam in the Garden of Eden, God is found *walking* with *Enoch*, as He had with Adam.

God still wanted the fellowship and companionship of the creature He had made in His own likeness.

Each of the other individuals cited were part of God's plan to make *direct access* to Himself a possibility for any human.

Noah was observed to be *the only person that God found in the entire population of the earth whose life was pleasing to Him.* The rottenness of sin had corrupted all of humanity, and God decided to wipe it all out, with the exception of Noah and his family. He sent a flood that completely enveloped the entire globe. Noah's descendants repopulated the earth, but sin was still embedded in the blood of the human race. Depravity, immorality, and debasement again became rampant.

Out of this morass of moral depravity, God selected *Abram* to be the father of a family that would eventually produce the final and definitive answer to the inherent problem between God and man.

> **"Now the LORD had said unto Abram, Get thee out of thy country, and from thy kindred, and from thy father's house, unto a land that I will shew thee: And <u>I will make of thee a great nation,</u> and I will bless thee, and make thy name great; and thou shalt be a blessing: And I will bless them that bless thee, and curse him that curseth thee: and <u>in thee shall all families of the earth be blessed.</u>"** (Genesis 12:13, AV)

Through an astounding array of fantastic miracles, including passing through the Red Sea on a pathway of dry land, the Israelites found themselves free from slavery. The Egyptian army was wiped out, and the Red Sea was filled again with water, separating them from the enemy. The nation that God promised was on the move!

Now that God had separated for Himself a group of people, He proceeded to educate them in His ways so that eventually, the fellowship that was intended from the beginning would be open to each and to all.

The first fact that had to be established was a huge gap that existed between God and man because of sin. Man had to realize that "God loved righteousness and hated iniquity."

To make this visually, emotionally, and mentally clear, God had the nation gather at the foot of Mount Sinai, in the middle of the desert, and made it unmistakable that no one was permitted to approach Him without acknowledging this fact. Anyone, except Moses and Aaron, that tried to approach His presence on the mountain would die immediately. He invited Moses to ascend the mountain to receive the terms upon which steps toward fellowship must be taken by the people.

> **"There shall not an hand touch it, but he shall surely be stoned, or shot through; whether it is beast or man, it shall not live: when the trumpet soundeth long, they shall come up to the mount. And Moses went down from the mount unto the people, and sanctified the people; and they washed their clothes. And he said unto the people, Be ready against the third day: come not at your wives. And it came to pass on the third day in the morning, that <u>there were thunders and lightnings, and a thick cloud upon the mount</u>, and the voice of the trumpet exceeding loud; so that all the <u>people that was in the camp trembled.</u> And Moses brought forth the people out of the camp to meet with God; and they stood at the nether part of the mount. And <u>mount Sinai was altogether on a smoke, because the LORD descended upon it in fire: and the smoke thereof ascended as the smoke of a furnace, and the whole mount quaked greatly.</u> And when the voice of the trumpet sounded long, and waxed louder and louder, Moses spake, and God answered him by a voice. And the LORD came down upon Mount Sinai, on the top of the mount: and the LORD called Moses up to the top of the mount; and Moses went up."** (Exodus 19:13-24:18, AV)

To clarify the basic requirement for any human to have a relationship with God, He stated this primary factor:

> **And God spoke all these words: "I am the LORD your God, who brought you out of Egypt, out of the land of slavery. <u>"You shall have no other gods before me. "You shall not make for yourself an idol in the form of anything in heaven above or on the earth beneath or in the waters below.</u> 5 You shall**

not bow down to them or worship them; for I, the LORD your God, am a jealous God," (Exodus 20:1-5, NIV84)

Since God had created all things in heaven and earth for His own glory, He made it obvious that under no circumstance would He tolerate anything or anyone that would supplant Him as the primary object of love in the human heart.

God issued to Moses the Ten Commandments, the outline of the statutes that would define the requirements to maintain open association between God and human, and human and human. They were followed by pages of detailed instructions on how to implement the principles of the Ten Commandments for daily use.

The Lord Jesus simplified the whole process when he answered the question of one of the religious rulers:

> **"One of them, an expert in the law, tested him with this question: 'Teacher, which is the greatest commandment in the Law?' Jesus replied: 'Love the Lord your God with all your heart and with all your soul and with all your mind.' This is the first and greatest commandment. And the second is like it: 'Love your neighbor as yourself.' All the Law and the Prophets hang on these two commandments."** (Matthew 22:35-40, NIV84)

The immediate future of the new nation was to be mobile in nature as they travelled to the Promised Land. God wanted the Israelites to know that His desire was to be with them day and night; therefore, He had Moses build a tent or tabernacle that would be placed in the midst of their encampment whenever they stopped and would go before them wherever they moved. The erection of the structure was described in great detail to Moses and was composed of the best material. An exceptionally brilliant artisan was endowed by God to supervise the erection of the house, where the force of God's presence would be experienced by the nation.

> **"Then have them make a sanctuary for me, and I will dwell among them. Make this tabernacle and all its furnishings**

exactly like the pattern I will show you." (Exodus 28:1-3, NIV84)

"Then the LORD said to Moses, "See, I have chosen Bezalel son of Uri, the son of Hur, of the tribe of Judah, and <u>I have filled him with the Spirit of God, with skill, ability and knowledge in all kinds of crafts</u>—to make artistic designs for work in gold, silver and bronze, to cut and set stones, to work in wood, and to engage in all kinds of craftsmanship." (Exodus 31:1-5, NIV84)

God's dealing with the *nation of Israel* was not only to teach *them* the components necessary to have a close relationship with Him, but it was a gigantic living object lesson for the succeeding generations of *all the peoples of the world.*

(BKC [OT] p. 147)

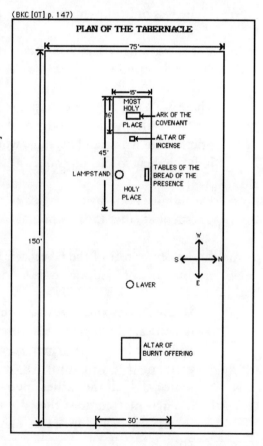

PLAN OF THE TABERNACLE

There are many lessons to be learned from the tabernacle and how it was to be used. For the purpose of emphasizing major points relating to our present consideration, the following are mentioned:

o   It was placed in the center of the nation, when they were camped, so that all would have the same access and be assured of the presence of God with them.

o   There was a fence surrounding the tent, which kept the people from directly approaching it.

o   There was only one entrance.

o   There was a daily sacrifice of two lambs, one in the morning and one in the evening.

o   There was a priest at the entrance to perform the necessary function for the petition of the individual to be presented to God. The priests were Aaron and his sons, who were dressed extravagantly to indicate their special position.

o   Death must occur by the slaying of an animal at the gate, before the priest could enter the compound on the behalf of the petitioner.

o   In the center rear of the tabernacle was the most holy place where the presence of God was to be found.

> **"Have Aaron your brother brought to you from among the Israelites, along with his sons Nadab and Abihu, Eleazar and Ithamar, <u>so they may serve me as priests. Make sacred garments for your brother Aaron</u>, to give him dignity and honor. Tell all the skilled men to whom I have given wisdom in such matters that they are to make garments for Aaron, for his consecration, so he may serve me as priest."** (Exodus 28:1-3, NIV84)

> **"This is what <u>you are to offer on the altar regularly each day: two lambs</u> a year old. Offer <u>one in the morning</u> and the <u>other at twilight</u>. With the first lamb offer a tenth of**

an ephah of fine flour mixed with a quarter of a hin of oil from pressed olives, and a quarter of a hin of wine as a drink offering. Sacrifice the other lamb at twilight with the same grain offering and its drink offering as in the morning—a pleasing aroma, an offering made to the LORD by fire. For the generations to come this burnt offering is to be made regularly at the entrance to the Tent of Meeting before the LORD. <u>There I will meet you and speak to you; there also I will meet with the Israelites, and the place will be consecrated by my glory. So I will consecrate the Tent of Meeting and the altar and will consecrate Aaron and his sons to serve me as priests.</u> Then I will dwell among the Israelites and be their God. They will know that <u>I am the LORD their God, who brought them out of Egypt so that I might dwell among them.</u> I am the LORD their God." (Exodus 29:38-46, NIV84)

"The LORD called to Moses and spoke to him from the Tent of Meeting. He said, 'Speak to the Israelites and say to them: '<u>When any of you brings an offering to the LORD,</u> bring as your offering an animal from either the herd or the flock. If the offering is a burnt offering from the herd, he is to offer a male without defect. <u>He must present it at the entrance to the Tent of Meeting so that it will be acceptable to the LORD. He is to lay his hand on the head of the burnt offering,</u> and it will be accepted on his behalf to make atonement for him. <u>He is to slaughter the young bull before the LORD,</u> and then Aaron's sons <u>the priests shall bring the blood and sprinkle it against the altar on all sides at the entrance to the Tent of Meeting.</u>'" (Leviticus 1:1-5, NIV84)

The picture we are given of the Israelites' access to the presence of God was complex and loathsome. God wanted personal and national acknowledgment of their sinfulness as they participated in a ritual that would dramatize and emphasize the horror, in God's eyes, of being short of His glory. Death was the penalty.

A substitute had to be presented and identification established by the placing of hands on the head of the animal by the individual (or the priest, in the case of the sacrifice being made on behalf of the nation). The blood of the animal must then be shed, causing death at the entrance of the fence around the tabernacle by the person concerned. The priest would then take the carcass into the enclosure on the behalf of the individual and present his case before the holy place.

Every morning and every evening, a lamb had to be slain to cover the people as a nation for the sins committed in between those periods of time.

> **"In fact, the law requires that nearly everything be cleansed with blood, and <u>without the shedding of blood there is no forgiveness</u>."** (Hebrews 9:22, NIV84)

The tabernacle and the rituals associated with it were predominate factors in the life of the nation, as they roamed in the wilderness for forty years prior to them entering the Promised Land.

When they crossed the Jordan River, the Ark of God preceded them, carried by the designated priests.

In the Ark of God were the tablets containing the Ten Commandments. Normally, when the tabernacle was erected, the position for the Ark of God was behind the veil, defining the most holy place. Only the priest could enter this space that signified the Presence of God.

> **"Joshua said to the Israelites, Come here and listen to the words of the LORD your God. This is how you will know that the living God is among you and that he will certainly drive out before you the Canaanites, Hittites, Hivites, Perizzites, Girgashites, Amorites and Jebusites. See, the ark of the covenant of the Lord of all the earth will go into the Jordan ahead of you."** (Joshua 3:9-11, NIV84)

Now the Ark of God, the presence of God, was going before them, leading them into a new venture. The Ark of God played an important role in the life of the Israeli nation during their motley occupation of the land. David finally consolidated the possession of the land and made Jerusalem its capital. His son, Solomon, was permitted by God to build a temple that featured the holiest place behind the veil in which was placed the Ark of God.

"When all the work Solomon had done for the temple of the LORD was finished, he brought in the things his father David had dedicated—the silver and gold and all the furnishings—and he placed them in the treasuries of God's temple. Then Solomon summoned to Jerusalem the elders of Israel, all the heads of the tribes and the chiefs of the Israelite families, to bring up the ark of the LORD's covenant from Zion, the City of David. And all the men of Israel came together to the king at the time of the festival in the seventh month. <u>When all the elders of Israel had arrived, the Levites took up the ark, and they brought up the ark and the Tent of Meeting and all the sacred furnishings in it. The priests, who were Levites, carried them up; and King Solomon and the entire assembly of Israel that had gathered about him were before the ark, sacrificing so many sheep and cattle that they could not be recorded or counted.</u>" (2 Chronicles 5:1-6, NIV84)

The temple stood until the Jews were defeated by the Babylonians, and the temple was destroyed at which time the Ark of the Covenant disappeared. The temple was rebuilt when the Jews were allowed to return to Jerusalem during the time of Cyrus, king of Persia.

"In the first year of Cyrus king of Persia, in order to fulfill the word of the LORD spoken by Jeremiah, the LORD moved the heart of Cyrus king of Persia to make a proclamation throughout his realm and to put it in writing:

This is what Cyrus king of Persia says:

'The LORD, the God of heaven, has given me all the kingdoms of the earth and <u>he has appointed me to build a temple for him at Jerusalem in Judah.</u> Anyone of his people among you—may his God be with him, and let him go up to Jerusalem in Judah and build the temple of the LORD, the God of Israel, the God who is in Jerusalem. And the people of any place where survivors may now be living are to provide him with silver and gold, with goods and livestock, and with

freewill offerings for the temple of God in Jerusalem.'" (Ezra 1:1-4, NIV84)

Herod the Great replaced this temple with one of his own making. This was the structure that existed at the time of Jesus's life on earth. Herod was a Roman political appointee, and he took this step as a means to please the Jewish leadership at the time.

At the beginning of the public activities of Jesus, we are given an indication of the next step that God was going to take to establish a permanent relationship between man and God. John the Baptist pointed to Jesus and said,

> **"The next day John saw Jesus coming toward him and said, <u>"Look, the Lamb of God, who takes away the sin of the world!</u> This is the one I meant when I said, 'A man who comes after me has surpassed me because he was before me.'"** (John 1:29-30, NIV84)

When Jesus died on the cross of Calvary, He took the place of each member of the human race. He became both the sacrifice and the priest who pled our case before the throne of God. The veil in the temple was torn, signifying that the final barrier separating unfettered fellowship between man and God was abolished. Anyone who would individually accept Christ's sacrifice and the atonement it represented for that person's sin would have total access to the Godhead.

> **"And when Jesus had cried out again in a loud voice, <u>he gave up his spirit. At that moment the curtain of the temple was torn in two from top to bottom.</u> The earth shook and the rocks split."** (Matthew 27:50-51, NIV84)

The writer to the Hebrews put it this way:

> **"First he said, 'Sacrifices and offerings, burnt offerings and sin offerings you did not desire, nor were you pleased with them' (although the law required them to be made). Then he said, 'Here I am, I have come to do your will.' He sets aside the first to establish the second. And by that will, <u>we have</u>**

been made holy through the sacrifice of the body of Jesus Christ once for all. Day after day every priest stands and performs his religious duties; again and again he offers the same sacrifices, which can never take away sins. But when this priest had offered for all time one sacrifice for sins, he sat down at the right hand of God. Since that time he waits for his enemies to be made his footstool, by one sacrifice he has made perfect forever those who are being made holy." (Hebrews 10:8-14, NIV84)

The temple and the sacrifices attached to it were no longer needed. There was not a requirement for a building or a specific place to meet with God because by His Spirit, He was everywhere and available anytime to believers whose sins had been cleansed by the shed blood of Jesus Christ. From that time until now, temples and church buildings are not a necessity. That is why Jesus said to the Samaritan woman:

> Jesus declared, 'Believe me, woman, a time is coming when you will worship the Father neither on this mountain nor in Jerusalem. You Samaritans worship what you do not know; we worship what we do know, for salvation is from the Jews. Yet a time is coming and has now come when the true worshipers will worship the Father in spirit and truth, for they are the kind of worshipers the Father seeks. God is spirit, and his worshipers must worship in spirit and in truth." (John 4:21-24, NIV84)

For decades, this woman's predecessors had been told that they must go to a specific location to worship, and now this concept had been completely wiped away by this One whom she had come to believe was the Messiah. Not only that, but He removed the requirement for physical paraphernalia to achieve recognition by God by stating that He was Spirit and worship of Him was only accepted on a spiritual basis.

What then does this mean, "spirit and truth"?

One of the meanings of "spirit" given in *Webster's New World Dictionary* is "the thinking, motivating, feeling part of man as distinguished from the body, mind, and intelligence of man."

Whatever one may think of the dictionary definition given above, it must be recognized that the "spirit" part of man's nature is something different from what may be termed as his soul, his id, or his ego. His "spirit" is the level at which communication takes place. The soul-id-ego level is where decision making is formulated.

An example of this concept can be had by visualizing a motivational speaker addressing a crowd and enthusiastically presenting a proposition that requires action of some sort by the listeners. His presentation is communicated in what we would call a "spirited" manner by use of his grammar, voice inflection, and body language. The people listen and refer the message to their "soul-ego-id" to take action or not. The communication medium was the spirit of the speaker to the spirit of the listener.

This activity is occurring constantly every day between created beings on greater or lesser levels of importance. The time it matters most is when it takes place between a human being and the Creator. Does the communication between the Spirit of God and the spirit of the person result in "truth" and "reality" worship? Or does it result in some phony physical activity or meaningless verbal rote in the expression of worship? Or is it totally ignored and dismissed?

> **"For the word of God is living and active. Sharper than any double-edged sword, it penetrates even to dividing soul and spirit, joints and marrow; it judges the thoughts and attitudes of the heart. Nothing in all creation is hidden from God's sight.** Everything is uncovered and lay bare before the eyes of him to whom we must give account. **Therefore, since we have a great high priest who has gone through the heavens, Jesus the Son of God,** let us hold firmly to the faith we profess. **For we do not have a high priest who is unable to sympathize with our weaknesses, but we have one who has been tempted in every way, just as we are—yet was without sin. Let us then approach the throne of grace with confidence, so that we**

may receive mercy and find grace to help us in our time of need." Hebrews 4:12-16, NIV84)

"**Now there have been many of those priests, since death prevented them from continuing in office; <u>because Jesus lives forever, he has a permanent priesthood.</u> Therefore <u>he is able to save completely those who come to God through him, because he always lives to intercede for them.</u>**" (Hebrews 7:23-25, NIV84)

"**And where these have been forgiven, there is no longer any sacrifice for sin. Therefore, brothers, <u>since we have confidence to enter the Most Holy Place by the blood of Jesus,</u> a new and living way opened for us through the curtain, that is, his body, <u>since we have a great priest over the house of God, let us draw near to God with a sincere heart</u> in full assurance of <u>faith,</u> having our hearts sprinkled to cleanse us from a guilty conscience and having our bodies washed with pure water.**" (Hebrews 10:18-22, NIV84)

These truths that were first pronounced to the ears of an unknown, unnamed, marred, and broken human, have reverberated through the halls of time for centuries to find the way to our ears today. How privileged we are to communicate with the Spirit of God through our spirits and to have the opportunity to enter the throne room of the God of the universe to speak with Him.

"**However, as it is written: 'No eye has seen, no ear has heard, no mind has conceived what God has prepared for those who love him'—but <u>God has revealed it to us by his Spirit. The Spirit searches all things, even the deep things of God.</u> For who among men knows the thoughts of a man except the man's spirit within him? In the same way no one knows the thoughts of God except the Spirit of God. We have not received the spirit of the world but the Spirit who is from God, that we may understand what God has freely given us. This is what we speak, not in words taught us by human wisdom but in words taught by the Spirit, expressing spiritual truths in spiritual words. The man without the Spirit** does not accept the things that come from the Spirit of God, for they are foolishness to him, and he cannot understand them, because they are spiritually discerned. The spiritual man makes judgments about all things, but he himself is not subject to any man's judgment: 'For who has known the mind of the Lord that he may instruct him?' <u>But we have the mind of Christ</u>." (1 Corinthians 2:9-16, NIV84)

Chapter 8

Is Jesus Christ God?

IF JESUS CHRIST is God, one would expect that He would demonstrate some characteristics that God alone possesses.

The apostle John seems to have an exceptionally close relationship with the Lord Jesus when he was on earth. He describes that relationship in 1 John 1:

> "That which was from the beginning, which we have heard, which we have seen with our eyes, which we have looked upon, and our hands have handled, of the Word of life; (For the life was manifested, and we have seen it, and bear witness, and shew unto you that eternal life, which was with the Father, and was manifested unto us;) That which we have seen and heard declare we unto you, that ye also may have fellowship with us: and truly our fellowship is with the Father, and with his Son Jesus Christ." (1 John 1, AV)

After traveling with Jesus for three years and observing Him on a daily basis, he was uniquely qualified to express an opinion about His Person. He was convinced that Jesus was indeed God. He states this unequivocally in the opening verses of his account of the life of Jesus, the Gospel of John:

> "Before anything else existed, there was Christ, with God. He has always been alive and is himself God. He created everything there is—nothing exists that he didn't make. Eternal life is in him, and this life gives light to all mankind. His life is the light that shines through the darkness—and the darkness can never extinguish it. God sent John the Baptist as a witness to the fact that Jesus Christ is the true Light. John himself was not the Light; he was only a witness to identify it. Later on, the one who is the true Light arrived

to shine on everyone coming into the world." (John 1:1-9, the Living Bible)

All but one of the absolute statements we contemplated in the last chapter of this document is a pronouncement from the pen of the apostle John: way, truth, life, love, light, and eternity. Of all of these attributes, the one that stands out is "life." Without "life" being in force, the others would not be required. John emphasized that Jesus is the life:

> "**Then spake Jesus again unto them, saying, <u>I am the light of the world</u>: he that followeth me shall not walk in darkness, but shall have <u>the light of life</u>.**" (John 8:12, AV)

> "<u>**I am come a light into the world**</u>**, that whosoever believeth on me should not abide in darkness.**" (John 12:46, AV)

Jesus Himself said that His *teachings* and His *miracles* are the credentials, which prove that He and God the Father are the same.

> "**Of course, <u>I have no need of human witnesses,</u> but I say these things so you might be saved. John (the Baptist) was like a burning and shining lamp, and you were excited for a while about his message. But I have <u>a greater witness than John</u>—my <u>teachings</u> and my <u>miracles</u>. The Father gave me these works to accomplish, and they prove that he sent me.**" (John 5:34-36, NIV84)

> "**For <u>as the Father hath life in himself</u>; so hath <u>he given to the Son to have life in himself</u>;**" (John 5:26, AV)

If "life" is the most outstanding attribute of God and Jesus Christ is God and His miracles are His credentials, we should expect to see this fact persuasively demonstrated during His days here on earth.

He demonstrated His control over *aquatic life*:

> "**Later Jesus appeared again to the disciples beside the Lake of Galilee. This is how it happened: A group of us were there—Simon Peter, Thomas, 'The Twin,' Nathanael from**

Cana in Galilee, my brother James and I and two other disciples. Simon Peter said, 'I'm going fishing.' 'We'll come too,' we all said. We did, but <u>caught nothing all night</u>. At dawn we saw a man standing on the beach but couldn't see who he was. He called, 'Any fish, boys?' 'No,' we replied. Then he said, '<u>Throw out your net on the right-hand side of the boat, and you'll get plenty of them!</u>' So <u>we did, and couldn't draw in the net because of the weight of the fish, there were so many!</u>" (John 21:1-6, the Living Bible)

He demonstrated His control over *plant life*:

"In the morning, as he was returning to Jerusalem, he was hungry and noticed a fig tree beside the road. He went over to see if there were any figs, but there were only leaves. Then he said to it, '<u>Never bear fruit again!</u>' And <u>soon the fig tree withered up.</u> The disciples were utterly amazed and asked, 'How did the fig tree wither so quickly?' Then Jesus told them, 'Truly, if you have faith and don't doubt, you can do things like this and much more. You can even say to this Mount of Olives, 'Move over into the ocean,' and it will. You can get anything you ask for in prayer—if you believe.'" (Matthew 21:18-22, the Living Bible)

He demonstrated His control over "*spirit*" and *animal life*:

"When they arrived at the other side of the lake, a demon-possessed man ran out from a graveyard, just as Jesus was climbing from the boat. This man lived among the gravestones and had such strength that whenever he was put into handcuffs and shackles—as he often was—he snapped the handcuffs from his wrists and smashed the shackles and walked away. No one was strong enough to control him. All day long and through the night he would wander among the tombs and in the wild hills, screaming and cutting himself with sharp pieces of stone. When Jesus was still far out on the water, the man had seen him and had run to meet him, and fell down before him. Then <u>Jesus spoke to the demon within the man and said, 'Come out, you evil spirit.'</u> It gave a terrible scream, shrieking, 'What are you going to do to me, Jesus, Son of the Most High God? For God's sake, don't torture me!' 'What is your name?' Jesus asked, and the demon replied, 'Legion, for <u>there are many of us here within this man.</u>' Then the demons begged him again and again not to send them to some distant land. Now as it happened there was a huge herd of hogs rooting around on the hill above the lake. <u>'Send us into those hogs,</u>' the demons begged. And Jesus gave them permission. Then <u>the evil spirits came out of the man and entered the hogs,</u> and <u>the entire herd plunged down the steep hillside into the lake and drowned.</u>" (Mark 5:1-13, the Living Bible)

He demonstrated His control over *young human life*:

"Not long afterwards Jesus went with his disciples to the village of Nain, with the usual great crowd at his heels. A funeral procession was coming out as he approached the village gate. <u>The boy who had died</u> was the only son of his widowed mother, and many mourners from the village were with her. When the Lord saw her, his heart overflowed with sympathy. 'Don't cry!' he said. <u>Then he walked over to the coffin and touched it, and the bearers stopped. 'Laddie,' he said, 'come back to life again.'</u> Then <u>the boy sat up and began to talk to those around him!</u> And Jesus gave him back to his mother. A great fear swept the crowd, and they exclaimed with praises to God, 'A mighty prophet has risen among us,' and, 'We have seen the hand of God at work today.' The report of what he did that day raced from end to end of Judea and even out across the borders." (Luke 7:11-18, the Living Bible)

In the dramatic resurrection of Lazarus, He demonstrated His power over *adult human life* even after life had ceased for many days:

"Do you remember Mary, who poured the costly perfume on Jesus' feet and wiped them with her hair? Well, her brother Lazarus, who lived in Bethany with Mary and her sister Martha, was sick. So the two sisters sent a message to

Jesus telling him, 'Sir, your good friend is very, very sick.' But when Jesus heard about it he said, 'The purpose of his illness is not death, but for the glory of God. I, the Son of God, will receive glory from this situation.' Although Jesus was very fond of Martha, Mary, and Lazarus, he stayed where he was for the next two days and made no move to go to them. Finally, after the two days, he said to his disciples, 'Let's go to Judea.' But his disciples objected. 'Master,' they said, 'only a few days ago the Jewish leaders in Judea were trying to kill you. Are you going there again?' Jesus replied, 'There are twelve hours of daylight every day, and during every hour of it a man can walk safely and not stumble. Only at night is there danger of a wrong step, because of the dark.' Then he said, 'Our friend Lazarus has gone to sleep, but now I will go and waken him!' The disciples, thinking Jesus meant Lazarus was having a good night's rest, said, 'That means he is getting better!' But Jesus meant Lazarus had died. Then he told them plainly, 'Lazarus is dead. And for your sake, I am glad I wasn't there, for this will give you another opportunity to believe in me. Come, let's go to him.' Thomas, nicknamed 'The Twin,' said to his fellow disciples, 'Let's go too—and die with him.'" (John 11:1-16, the Living Bible)

"But some said, 'This fellow healed a blind man—why couldn't he keep Lazarus from dying?' And again Jesus was moved with deep anger. Then they came to the tomb. It was a cave with a heavy stone rolled across its door. 'Roll the stone aside,' Jesus told them. But Martha, the dead man's sister, said, 'By now the smell will be terrible, for he has been dead four days.' 'But didn't I tell you that you will see a wonderful miracle from God if you believe?' Jesus asked her. So they rolled the stone aside. Then Jesus looked up to heaven and said, 'Father, thank you for hearing me. (You always hear me, of course, but I said it because of all these people standing here, so that they will believe you sent me.)' Then he shouted, 'Lazarus, come out!' And Lazarus came—bound up in the gravecloth, his face muffled in a head swath. Jesus told them, 'Unwrap him and let him go!'

And <u>so at last many of the Jewish leaders</u> who were with Mary and <u>saw it happen, finally believed on him.</u> But some went away to the Pharisees and reported it to them." (John 11:37-46, the Living Bible)

The greatest demonstration that Jesus Christ was indeed God, was the yielding of His own life and taking it up again, His death and resurrection:

"Then saith he to the disciple, Behold thy mother! And from that hour that disciple took her unto his own home. After this, Jesus <u>knowing that all things were now accomplished,</u> that the scripture might be fulfilled, saith, I thirst. Now there was set a vessel full of vinegar: and they filled a spunge with vinegar, and put it upon hyssop, and put it to his mouth. When Jesus therefore had received the vinegar, <u>he said, It is finished: and he bowed his head, and gave up the ghost.</u>" (John 19:27-30, AV)

"Now in the place where he was crucified there was a garden; and in the garden a new sepulchre, wherein was never man yet laid. There laid they Jesus therefore because of the Jews' preparation day; for the sepulchre was nigh at hand." (John 19:41-42, AV)

"We went on home, and by that time Mary had returned to the tomb and was standing outside crying. And as she wept, she stooped and looked in and saw two white-robed angels sitting at the head and foot of the place where the body of Jesus had been lying. 'Why are you crying?' the angels asked her. 'Because they have taken away my Lord,' she replied, 'and I don't know where they have put him.' She glanced over her shoulder and saw someone standing behind her. <u>It was Jesus, but she didn't recognize him!</u> 'Why are you crying?' he asked her. 'Whom are you looking for?' She thought he was the gardener. 'Sir,' she said, 'if you have taken him away, tell me where you have put him, and I will go and get him.' <u>'Mary!' Jesus said. She turned toward him.</u> 'Master!' she exclaimed." (John 20:10-16, the Living Bible)

"One of the disciples, Thomas, 'The Twin,' was not there at the time with the others. <u>When they kept telling him, 'We have seen the Lord,' he replied, 'I won't believe it unless I see the nail wounds in his hands—and put my fingers into them—and place my hand into his side.'</u> Eight days later the disciples were together again, and this time <u>Thomas was with them.</u> The doors were locked; but suddenly, as before, <u>Jesus was standing among them and greeting them. Then he said to Thomas, 'Put your finger into my hands. Put your hand into my side. Don't be faithless any longer. Believe!' 'My Lord and my God!' Thomas said.</u>" (John 20:24-28, the Living Bible)

The ultimate test to prove that Jesus is God and that He is *life* is that he controls life in all its forms. There were many other miracles that were wrought by Jesus, but these are amplified because life is the paramount factor basic to everything else there is. If there is no life, anything else is meaningless.

> <u>"I am come that they might have life, and that they might have it more abundantly."</u> (John 10:10, AV)

Chapter 9

If God Be for Us, Who Can Be against Us?

I N OTHER WORDS, if we are on God's side, who could possibly destroy us? The utmost in safety and security is ours.

In chapter 6, we considered seven basic features that the Bible says that are fundamentally found in the character of God. It is the combination of those components that provide the children of God their sanctuary.

1. God is the *Way* of salvation. Therefore, we can escape the ravages and punishment of sin. We do not have to rely on earning our salvation by our own good works.

   "For the wages of sin is death, but the <u>free gift of God</u> is eternal life <u>through Jesus Christ our Lord</u>." (Romans 6:23, the Living Bible)

2. God is the *Truth*. The fact is that in reality, God is in control of all the governments that ever assumed power in the history of the world. The fact is that God is the source of all energy and knowledge. Nothing can happen to the child of God on earth, unless it is permitted by Him.

   "By my great power I have made the earth and all mankind and every animal; and I give these things of mine to anyone I want to." (Jeremiah 27:5, the Living Bible)

3. God is *Life*. God gives and maintains the life on earth that He has provided to every human being. During that life on earth, each person is given the option to receive or reject eternal life, which is unending association with God. This gives the believer the

confidence to know that the worst that can happen, results in the best that can happen.

"I have written this to you who believe in the Son of God <u>so that you may know you have eternal life</u>." (1 John 5:13, the Living Bible)

4. God is *Light*. God is in control of all knowledge and physical energy. Therefore anything that occurs of a physical nature will result to the ultimate benefit of the believer.

"He has showered down upon us the richness of his grace—for how well he understands us and <u>knows what is best for us at all times</u>." (Ephesians 1:8, the Living Bible)

5. God is *Love*. Love is the force that binds together the relationship between all living beings. Without love, the attachment between God and man could not have happened.

"But God, who is rich in mercy, <u>for his great love wherewith he loved us, Even when we were dead in sins, hath quickened us together with Christ,</u> (by grace ye are saved;) And hath raised us up together, and made us sit together in heavenly places in Christ Jesus: That in the ages to come he might shew the exceeding riches of his grace in his kindness toward us through Christ Jesus." (Ephesians 2:4-7, AV)

6. God is *the Beginning and the End*. If God incorporates the beginning and the end, it is tantamount to saying that He is Eternity. This means that the association of the believer with Him is unlimited.

"For our light affliction, which is but for a moment, worketh for us a far more exceeding and eternal weight of glory; while we look not at the things which are seen, but at the things which are not seen: for <u>the things which are seen are temporal; but the things which are not seen are eternal</u>." (2 Corinthians 4:17-18, AV)

7. God is a *Consuming Fire*. We have considered that this demonstrates that God, "the Judge of all the earth," will clear out all in the universe that has defied Him. He will prepare a place for all who have loved Him and entered His family.

> "Let not your heart be troubled: ye believe in God, believe also in me. In my Father's house are many mansions: if it were not so, I would have told you. <u>I go to prepare a place for you. And if I go and prepare a place for you, I will come again, and receive you unto myself; that where I am, there ye may be also.</u>" (John 14:1-3, AV)

> "<u>There shall be nothing in the city that is evil;</u> for the throne of God and of the Lamb will be there, and his servants will worship him. And they shall see his face; and his name shall be written on their foreheads." (Revelation 22:3-4, the Living Bible)

The apostle Paul presents a powerful summary of the subject:

> "<u>What can we ever say to such wonderful things as these? If God is on our side, who can ever be against us?</u> Since he did not spare even his own Son for us but gave him up for us all, won't he also surely give us everything else? Who dares accuse us whom God has chosen for his own? Will God? No! He is the one who has forgiven us and given us right standing with himself. Who then will condemn us? Will Christ? No! For he is the one who died for us and came back to life again for us and is sitting at the place of highest honor next to God, pleading for us there in heaven. Who then can ever keep Christ's love from us? When we have trouble or calamity, when we are hunted down or destroyed, is it because he doesn't love us anymore? And <u>if we are hungry or penniless or in danger or threatened with death, has God deserted us? No, for the Scriptures</u> <u>tell us that for his sake we must be ready to face death at every moment of the day</u>—we are like sheep awaiting slaughter; but <u>despite all this, overwhelming victory is ours through Christ</u> who loved us enough to die for us. <u>For I am convinced that nothing</u>

can ever separate us from his love. Death can't, and life can't. The angels won't, and all the powers of hell itself cannot keep God's love away. Our fears for today, our worries about tomorrow, or where we are—high above the sky, or in the deepest ocean—nothing will ever be able to separate us from the love of God demonstrated by our Lord Jesus Christ when he died for us." (Romans 8:31-39, the Living Bible)

Chapter 10

How Should We Respond?

HUMAN BEINGS ARE bags of skin into which a collection of bones, organs, tubes, wiring, and a command center have been placed. The ingredients have been miraculously assembled so that there are arms, legs, hands, and muscles that are sustained by a system of pipes, which distribute chemicals that have been produced by a series of organs.

All this and more are under the control of an "engineer" implanted somewhere in the mix. The "engineer" has been termed many things, soul, spirit, ego, self, etc. Whatever the name that is chosen to call the implant, the moment of the insertion is the moment of the breath of life, similar to the Creator breathing upon Adam, the first human.

Little by little, the "engineer" controls the activities of the apparatus within the "skin" into which he has been positioned. He has been given a free will to make decisions, the ability to hear, to see, to think, and to take actions in the environment into which his "skin" has been placed.

The Great Creator, who gave the "engineer" a chance at life, has a loving interest in every move he makes. The actions of the "engineer" are measured and assessed by two factors: (1) does he love the Creator?; and (2) does he love the other "engineers" in the other "bags of skin" among whom he moves and lives and works?

The Bible gives an in-depth description of the above thoughts:

> **"You made all the delicate, inner parts of my body and knit them together in my mother's womb. Thank you for making me so wonderfully complex! It is amazing to think about. Your workmanship is marvelous—and how well I know it. You were there while I was being formed in utter seclusion! You saw me before I was born** and scheduled each day of

my life before I began to breathe. Every day was recorded in your book! <u>How precious it is, Lord, to realize that you are thinking about me constantly!</u> I can't even count how many times a day your thoughts turn toward me. And when I waken in the morning, you are still thinking of me!" (Psalm 139:13-18, the Living Bible)

"<u>For the eyes of the Lord search back and forth across the whole earth, looking for people whose hearts are perfect toward him, so that he can show his great power in helping them.</u> (2 Chronicles 16:9, the Living Bible)

"'Sir, which is the most important command in the laws of Moses?' Jesus replied, 'Love the Lord your God with all your heart, soul, and mind.' This is the first and greatest commandment. The second most important is similar: '<u>Love your neighbor as much as you love yourself.</u>' All the other commandments and all the demands of the prophets stem from these two laws and are fulfilled if you obey them. <u>Keep only these and you will find that you are obeying all the others.</u>" (Matthew 22:36-40, the Living Bible)

When we review the magnificence, the majesty, the might, the gentleness, the loving care, the generosity, and the personal interest the God of the universe has shown to each little "engineer," He has honored him with the gift of life in a "bag of skin." And the promise of boundless life when the "bag of skin" must be left behind and its resident introduced to eternity, what would one expect God to anticipate as our gift to Him? Everything?

That is what the apostle Paul recommends that we do. Our whole "bag of skin" that He has given us should be presented to Him as an offering!

"And so, dear brothers, I plead with you to <u>give your bodies to God. Let them be a living sacrifice,</u> holy—the kind he can accept. <u>When you think of what he has done for you, is this too much to ask?</u> Don't copy the behavior and customs of this world, but be a new and different person with a fresh newness in all you do and think. Then <u>you will learn from your own experience how his ways will really satisfy you.</u> As

God's messenger I give each of you God's warning: <u>Be honest in your estimate of yourselves,</u> measuring your value by how much faith God has given you. Just as there are many parts to our bodies, so it is with Christ's body. We are all parts of it, and <u>it takes every one of us to make it complete, for we each have different work to do. So we belong to each other,</u> and each needs all the others. <u>God has given each of us the ability to do certain things well.</u> So if God has given you the ability to prophesy, then prophesy whenever you can—as often as your faith is strong enough to receive a message from God. If your gift is that of serving others, serve them well. If you are a teacher, do a good job of teaching. If you are a preacher, see to it that your sermons are strong and helpful. If God has given you money, be generous in helping others with it. If God has given you administrative ability and put you in charge of the work of others, take the responsibility seriously. Those who offer comfort to the sorrowing should do so with Christian cheer. <u>Don't just pretend that you love others: really love them.</u> Hate what is wrong. Stand on the side of the good. Love each other with brotherly affection and take delight in honoring each other. Never be lazy in your work, <u>but serve the Lord enthusiastically. Be glad for all God is planning for you.</u> Be patient in trouble, and prayerful always. When God's children are in need, you be the one to help them out. And get into the habit of inviting guests home for dinner or, if they need lodging, for the night. If someone mistreats you because you are a Christian, don't curse him; pray that God will bless him. When others are happy, be happy with them. If they are sad, share their sorrow. Work happily together. <u>Don't try to act big. Don't try to get into the good graces of important people, but enjoy the company of ordinary folks. And don't think you know it all!</u> Never pay back evil for evil. Do things in such a way that everyone can see you are honest clear through. Don't quarrel with anyone. Be at peace with everyone, just as much as possible. Dear friends, <u>never avenge yourselves. Leave that to God, for he has said that he will repay those who deserve it. Don't take the law into your own hands.</u> Instead, feed your enemy if he is hungry. If he is thirsty give him something to drink and you will be "heaping coals of fire on his head." In other words, he will feel ashamed of himself for what he has done to you. Don't let evil get the upper hand, but <u>conquer evil by doing good.</u>" (Romans 12:1-21, the Living Bible)

Not all the ingredients in the "bags of skin" are the same. Some have bigger and brighter brains, some have more artistic qualities, some are more business oriented, some have flexible muscles and are more athletic, and some have an assortment of these and other abilities. All have been given by the Creator. There is nothing we have that has not been given to us. Each "engineer" is called upon to assess, evaluate, and prioritize his inventory of attributes.

Then comes the point of how and for whom the gifts are to be utilized. Will it be for self-aggrandizement or for God and others? Will it be given out of sincere love or shallow pretense? Will it be for show and to try to act big?

"But remember this—<u>if you give little, you will get little.</u> A farmer who plants just a few seeds will get only a small crop." (2 Corinthians 9:6)

"<u>If he sows to please his own wrong desires, he will be planting seeds of evil and he will surely reap a harvest of spiritual decay and death;</u> but <u>if he plants the good things of the Spirit, he will reap the everlasting life that the Holy Spirit gives him.</u>" (Galatians 6:8, the Living Bible)

"Don't be misled; remember that you can't ignore God and get away with it: <u>a man will always reap just the kind of crop he sows!</u>" (Galatians 6:7, the Living Bible)

Chapter 11

Postscript

THE SUBJECT MATTER we have contemplated in this book is the most important that the human mind can address. It seems to me.

I have had my ninetieth birthday this year. As time is currently measured, I have had a long life. When one approaches the end of one's time on earth, there is the inclination to evaluate what activities have been of greater or less significance.

Because of illnesses and advancing age, my physical participation has been substantially suppressed, which in turn has reduced my ability to "get out and around." As a consequence, I have spent most of the last two to three years at home, alone for the most part. At first, this seemed disastrous.

I had always been a very active person, including pursuits which I considered to be Christian service. I was hounded by the thought "What can I possibly do now that will be of any import? I have nothing left to give."

My thoughts led me to ask, "What does God want most?" Of course, He makes it clear in the first commandment: "Love the Lord your God with all your heart." I certainly had a long way to go to come near that goal. My life had been busy with doing things for Him, great gaps when I ignored Him completely, and others when I was just busy. Very little of the total time had been in His presence, soaking up who He really is . . . in a word, "worship."

I now have been given a marvelous period of time to meditate, which perhaps will be the most blessed phase of my life.

This whole episode in my own history has made the story of Martha and Mary come alive to me in an impelling realistic manner:

"As Jesus and the disciples continued on their way to Jerusalem they came to a village where a woman named Martha welcomed them into her home. Her sister Mary sat on the floor, listening to Jesus as he talked. But Martha was the jittery type and was worrying over the big dinner she was preparing. She came to Jesus and said, 'Sir, doesn't it seem unfair to you that my sister just sits here while I do all the work? Tell her to come and help me.' But the Lord said to her, 'Martha, dear friend, you are so upset over all these details! <u>There is really only one thing worth being concerned about.</u> <u>Mary has discovered it—and I won't take it away from her!</u>'" (Luke 10:38-42, the Living Bible)

I guess at this stage of one's life, it is natural to ask, "What would I do differently?" There are many minor things, but the two most important ones are as follows:

1. I would more carefully and extensively evaluate (including participate in a discussion with others) what my particular talents are and how best to use them.

2. I would spend more time alone with God, being saturated with who He is (walking with Him as Enoch did). The broad sweep of the personality and power of God leaves me stunned, aghast, and frightened to approach Him. However, He brushes aside those fears and says, "Just call me Father." In today's parlance, that would be "Dad."

To help me embrace this unfathomable relationship, I personalize the Lord's Prayer and Psalm 23.

"After this manner therefore pray ye: <u>My</u> Father which art in heaven, Hallowed be thy name. Thy kingdom come. Thy will be done in earth, as it is in heaven. Give <u>me</u> this day <u>my</u> daily bread. And forgive <u>me</u> <u>my</u> debts, as <u>I</u> forgive my debtors. And lead <u>me</u> not into temptation, but deliver <u>me</u> from evil: For thine is the kingdom, and the power, and the glory, forever. Amen." (Matthew 6:9-13, AV)

A Psalm of David

"The LORD is _my_ shepherd; _I_ shall not want. He maketh _me_ to lie down in green pastures: he leadeth _me_ beside the still waters. He restoreth _my_ soul: he leadeth _me_ in the paths of righteousness for his name's sake. Yea, though _I_ walk through the valley of the shadow of death, _I_ will fear no evil: for thou art with _me_; thy rod and thy staff they comfort _me_. Thou preparest a table before _me_ in the presence of mine enemies: thou anointest _my_ head with oil; _my_ cup runneth over. Surely goodness and mercy shall follow _me_ all the days of _my_ life: and _I_ will dwell in the house of the LORD forever." (Psalm 23, AV)

About the Author

D AVID WILSON WAS born in Kearny NJ, USA February 24, 1922.

His father's business took the family to Toronto, Ontario, Canada when he was 12 years of age.

At nineteen he enlisted in the US Navy (after the attack on Pearl Harbor) where he served 3 ½ years in anti-submarine warfare and LSM flotilla 11 during WWII.

After the war he graduated from Emmaus Bible School upon completing three years of intensive systematic study of the Bible. He became a pastor of a church, and the director of a children's summer camp in the Province of Quebec for approximately 10 years.

Camp Mini Yo We, a children's camp, which he had help start in Ontario immediately after the war, became so successful that it required a full time manager. David was offered the opportunity and he accepted.

After returning to Toronto and living in Ontario for several years, he became interested in national politics which lead to a senior position in one of the political parties in Ottawa. Other politically related occupations followed.

Because of business and personal reasons he has travelled extensively in North America. He has also visited many other parts of the world.

He has been exposed to various social environments having lived in three major cities, two small towns and one rural setting

He is a widower, the father of four children, the grandfather of four children and the great grandfather of three great grandchildren.

In 1968 he moved his residence to Vancouver, BC, where he managed a real estate sales office for many years, combined with a personal program of general volunteer hospital visitation plus participating in the hospice program for the City of Vancouver.

At time of writing he has had ninety birthdays. Consequently he has a deep well of broad personal life involvements from which to draw. His experiences encompass, a youth in the years of the great depression, a sailor in WWII, events surrounding a pastor's life, the tough times as a businessman and compassionate moments in hospice settings. He would like to share, with his readers, the reliability and faithfulness of God throughout the years.

CPSIA information can be obtained at www.ICGtesting.com
Printed in the USA
LVOW041934170912

299183LV00001B/2/P